DANCING IN ALL AGES

BY

EDWARD SCOTT

AUTHOR OF
"DANCING" (DOUBLE VOLUME) IN THE "ALL ENGLAND" SERIES
ETC.

LONDON

SWAN SONNENSCHEIN & CO., LIM.
PATERNOSTER SQUARE

1899

PREFACE

IN writing the following pages, it has been my
endeavour to furnish some information concerning the practice of dancing which has not hitherto
found a place in treatises upon the subject. To the
dances of barbarous countries and primitive tribes
my attention has not here been given. I have
briefly traced the rise, progress, and, I fear it must
be added, decline of the art among certain civilised
nations from the earliest ages to our own times.
So far as my memory would allow, acknowledgment
has in all cases been made of the sources whence
facts have been obtained, or authors have been cited
in whose works a verification of statements may be
found; but, of course, for deductions drawn therefrom, and views advanced, unless otherwise specified,
I am myself responsible.

For information respecting the ancients, and their
manner of dancing, I have frequently consulted the
works of Herodotus, Plato, Xenophon, Aristophanes,

Athenæus, Pausanias, the Roman historians, and, somewhat warily, Lucian. Among modern authors, I am indebted to Wilkinson, Birch, Rawlinson, Müller, and Donaldson; while the technical writers who have afforded the greatest assistance are, I think, Jehan Tabouret, Rameau, and Noverre. The above-mentioned, however, are only a few among many authors, ancient and modern, to whom due acknowledgment is made in the text. To the observant reader it will also be evident that much information has been gathered from the study of sculptures, pottery, pictures, and other archæological and modern exhibits to be found in museums and art galleries both at home and abroad.

Unlike my predecessors in this field of research, I have adopted the plan of keeping distinct and considering separately the dances of each of the great nations of antiquity, and have described them, so far as was practicable, in chronological order. This course certainly renders the work more convenient for purposes of reference, and also, I venture to think, of greater interest to the general reader— an interest which it has been my endeavour to enhance by the introduction of appropriate anecdotes and stories.

I should perhaps mention that the earlier chapters of the present work were begun some years since with a view to their being incorporated with a practical treatise on dancing, now published as a double volume in the All England Series of Hand-books. The historical aspects of the art, however, possess considerable interest for the author, and the work soon grew to larger proportions than was at first anticipated. Accordingly I decided to keep the historical and critical chapters distinct from those purely practical, and eventually produce them as a separate and complete volume.

This task, which was set aside for a while, has now been resumed in the belief that, being written on entirely different lines, the present work will not in any way clash with existing volumes. It will be noticed by those who have perused the agreeable pages, for which Mrs. Groves is chiefly responsible, that although a somewhat wide geographical range is covered by her research, all that she has to say about the dances of ancient Egypt, Greece, and Rome is contained in a very few pages, and that but little information is given concerning the most famous dances of modern times. I believe that for the present work, so far as it goes, I may fairly

claim greater thoroughness and accuracy of detail
than has hitherto been found in historical treatises
on dancing. Moreover, when writers on this subject frankly confess to having no practical knowledge
thereof, it would seem that there is sufficient room
for the critical and descriptive efforts of those who,
in addition to literary research, have made a conscientious study of the art in theory and practice.

EDWARD SCOTT,

ROCHESTER HOUSE, ROCHESTER GARDENS,
        WEST BRIGHTON,
    AND LONDON.

CONTENTS

DANCING IN ALL AGES

CHAPTER I.

THE NATURE AND ORIGIN OF DANCING.

A S a spontaneous expression of emotion by bodily action, dancing must have existed from the remotest ages. Its true source lies in the nature of our organism. Sudden or intense excitement causes a more than usually rapid oxidation of brain tissue, and physical exertion is the natural outlet by which the overcharged brain is relieved. For this reason a child jumps with delight when informed of a pleasure in store for him. Savages are in many respects like children, and express their feelings in a similar manner, often executing wild dances without order or design. If, then, it were possible for us to travel back to those "unhappy far-off times" before the dawn of civilisation, when palæolithic man first

B

cooked his food in a hole dug in the ground and filled with water and hot stones, doubtless we should find him executing an improvised dance of delight around his primitive cauldron as he watched the seething liquid in anticipation of the delicacy he was about to enjoy.

But the capacity for this kind of dancing, which results from excess of vitality, is by no means confined to human beings. It is shared by many animals. A dog dances with delight when he sees his master; a horse prances to the sound of music; there are birds that dance; and of young lambs Thomson, in his "Castle of Indolence," sings,—

> "Rampant with life, their joy all joy exceeds,
> Yet what but high-strung health this dancing pleasure
> breeds?"

Natural dancing, which is merely a vigorous leaping motion of the body under the influence of suddenly awakened sensibility, is not, however, the kind of dancing that we are about to consider in the following pages. It is only the original from which the movements hereafter to be described have developed. The *act* of dancing can in no sense be regarded as man's invention; it belongs to his nature. In its infancy, so to speak, dancing probably consisted of nothing more than a heterogeneous mixture of steps and jumps, for, as Athenæus observes, "the motion of the feet was adopted long before there was any motion of the hands."* It is only the dancing that, to borrow Grote's expression, has been "transferred from the field of spontaneous nature to the garden of art," dancing that is subject to definite rules, that can properly be regarded as the invention of man.

And now, before proceeding further, let us pause to consider what it is that really constitutes dancing in the generally accepted sense of the term. In the course of my life I have found opportunities to peruse many books bearing directly or indirectly upon the subject, books both ancient and modern; but I do not remember ever to have come across a satisfactory explanation of the difference between what we, by common tacit consent, understand as dancing, and other bodily movements. Where so many others have failed, I too am likely to fail; but, all the same, I will endeavour to make the difference clear.

It is quite usual to define dancing as being a

* *Deipnosophists*, lib. xiv. 28.

rhythmical movement of the body regulated by
music. This is all very well so far as it goes, but
such a definition obviously includes walking or
marching in measured steps to the accompaniment
of some melody. The difficulty of framing a suitable definition is apparent when we consider that
the movements employed in dancing are all framed
upon our three natural means of locomotion: walking, running, and jumping. Even the most com-
plicated steps are framed upon natural movements
accompanied by turnings of the body, but many
graceful dances consist merely of actions similar
to those we employ in every-day life. What,
then, constitutes the difference between running,
walking, leaping, and dancing? It is not the
accompaniment of music, or even the employment
of rhythm, for we may run, walk, or jump in
rhythmic measure, and in time to music, and yet
our movements may not appear like dancing; while
a dance will still appear to be such, even if un-
accompanied by the sound of music. As in the
Witches' Chorus, we may "dance to the echoes of
our feet."

My own idea of the matter is this: A succession
of running steps, of walking steps, or of leaps, even

if rhythmical, does not involve to any appreciable extent the employment of the mental faculties. The action of the limbs is not regulated by conscious volition. But should these several steps be combined and alternated in some regular sequence, and we take, say, first a walking step, then a running step, and finally a jump, in order to repeat these the faculty of memory is called into requisition; the movement becomes a studied movement, and partakes of the character of dancing. But we associate the idea of dancing with the idea of gracefulness, and it may be urged that a wholly spontaneous movement, or combination of movements, will often appear exceedingly graceful. This may be so, but such movements, if apparently spontaneous, are generally the result of past training; and, in any case, movements that convey the impression of dancing will be movements that could not be repeated exactly by the performer or imitated by another person without some mental effort.*

* It is a gross libel on the votaries of Terpsichore to aver, as some do, that "the biggest fools make the best dancers." Teachers of the art know by experience that such is not the case.

Bearing these things in mind, I think, then, we may provisionally define dancing in its simplest form as

A rhythmic progression of the body by varied and studied actions of the limbs.

This definition applies to any form of dancing, recreative or otherwise. A somewhat higher form may be defined as

A rhythmic motion or progression of the body by varied and studied actions of the limbs, combined with movements and attitudes arranged for the avowed purpose of displaying agility and personal gracefulness.

The above may apply to purely artistic as well as recreative dancing; but dramatic dancing in its highest form is

The art of expressing gracefully and intelligibly, by movement and gesture, every emotion and sentiment of which the mind is capable, and every incident possible to human life.

Such, for instance, was the wonderful pantomimic dancing of the Greeks. It is to such dancing that Mr. Pater alludes in his essay on Lacedæmon, when he says, "With no movement of voice or hand or foot unconsidered, as Plato forbids, it was the

perfect flower of their correction of that minute
patience and care which ends in a perfect ex-
pressiveness; not a note, a glance, a touch, but told
obediently in the promotion of a firmly grasped
mental conception, as in that perfect poetry, or
sculpture, or painting, in which the finger of the
master is in every part of his work." * Such was
the dancing whose execution, we are told by Lucian,
required almost universal knowledge on the part of
the artiste. It was the dancing of Telestes, of
Pylades and Bathyllus, and of Roscius, who, it is
stated, in a friendly contest with Cicero succeeded
in expressing more by gesture than the orator was
able to express by word of mouth.† There has been
nothing like it in modern times, although Noverre
would appear to have been almost as exacting in his
enumeration of the necessary qualifications of a good
ballet-master as was Lucian of old. "As for the
ballet itself," said he, "it should through the eyes

---

* *Contemporary Review*, June, 1892.

† The pantomimists who maintained their reputation from the
age of Augustus to the sixth century expressed without the use of
words the various fables of the gods and heroes of antiquity; and
the perfection of their art, which sometimes disarmed the gravity
of the philosophers, always excited the applause and wonder of
the people.—GIBBON'S *Decline and Fall*, chap. xxxi.

speak, as it were, to the very soul of the spectator.
Explanatory speeches will be useless. A mute but
powerful eloquence will be substituted to much
better effect. Each motion will be a sentence, every
attitude will betray a situation, each gesture convey
a thought, each glance a new sentiment, and every
part will please because the whole will be a faithful
imitation of nature."

Perhaps the nearest approach to the pantomimic
dancing of ancient times that we have seen of late
was exhibited some years since in the beautiful and
refined ballet called *Excelsior*. I speak of this
ballet as I saw it performed on the Continent; but
it was, I believe, also exhibited at Her Majesty's
Theatre in London. Still later we have had the
clever wordless drama entitled *L'Enfant Prodigue*.
This, perhaps, was something like the mimetic
dancing of the Greeks, which they introduced
occasionally into their *hyporchema*. But all Greek
dancing was not purely expressive. Quick steps
and lively movements of the arms were sometimes
employed, as in the Italian tarentella,* and we read
in the Homeric hymn how Apollo led the dance with
"grand and lofty steps."

* *Vide* Dr. DONALDSON's *Theatre of the Greeks.*

I have pointed out that, although the *act* of dancing may be said to have its origin in man's nature, as a regulated art dancing, like music, may certainly be regarded as an invention. But who the inventor really was is, of course, a matter of the merest conjecture. The ancients naturally attributed the invention of an art which they held in the greatest respect, and associated with all that was most sacred, to some divinity or immortal hero. In the *Ajax* of Sophocles the god Pan is spoken of as a dancing-master, Phœbus is called by Pindar the "prince of dancers," and even the mighty Jove has, according to Athenæus, been represented by Eumelius as "moving gracefully amidst the dancing throng." It has been said that the goddess Cybele or Rhea was the first teacher of the art, and that when she entrusted the care of her infant Zeus to the Curates she imparted to them a warlike dance, accompanied by the clashing of shields and cymbals, by which means they succeeded in drowning the child's cries and concealing his whereabouts from his greedy old father, Chronos or Saturn, who would otherwise have devoured him as he did the rest of his sons.

It has been suggested that the muse Erato, who

invented marriage, also invented dancing. Some
say that the Egyptian Mercury or Thoth was the
originator of the art, others that it was instituted
by the Dioscuri; and we are told that Theseus
when returning from Crete, being driven on the
coast of Delos, taught the youths of that island a
dance representing the various windings of the
labyrinth from which, after slaying the Minotaur,
he had escaped by the clew of thread given to him
by the fair Ariadne.

All this, however, is so closely connected with
mere fable that my only excuse for giving it
place in these pages must be the same which the
ancient historian Herodotus pleads when he tells
some of his more than usually improbable anecdotes:
that he doesn't believe a word of the story he is
narrating himself, but perhaps a reader may be
found who is willing to give it credit. At least, as
Artemus Ward would say, he uses "words to that
effect."

But before taking leave of the purely hypothetical
originators of dancing, of whom only a few have here
been mentioned, I should not, in common fairness
to the avowed enemies of the art, omit to state that
its invention has not unfrequently been ascribed to

the presiding genius of a place which, with the exception of the circle to which Dante consigns Ugolino and Ruggieri, we are not accustomed to associate with the idea of extreme cold. This hypothesis, however, would only lead a lover of dancing to endorse the opinion sometimes expressed that the personage in question cannot be quite "so black as he is painted," or surely he would never have imparted to mankind so beneficial and beautiful an art.

It seems to me that the ancients were far more consistent in supposing that the inhabitants of Olympus were the inventors and first teachers of dancing. But if we descend from the regions of romance, and occupy ourselves with the investigation of sober historical facts, we shall find that, although the real origin of dancing as a cultivated art is involved in an obscurity which no ingenuity of research is able to dispel, there can at least be no possible doubt of its very great antiquity.

Among the Greeks poetry, music, and dancing were inseparable arts. The poets themselves set music to their own verses, and we may infer that they were always sung, or perhaps it may be

more accurate to say chanted, for it is certain that
long odes could not have been sung to any com-
plicated arrangement of melody. Whatever the
music of the ancients may have been—and Dr.
Burney, who had devoted years to the inquiry, is
reported to have confessed to a friend that he
"never understood Greek music or found anyone else who did understand it"—it is absolutely
certain that it must have been music of a very
different nature from ours. For one thing, instead
of employing two modes, major and minor, as we
do, they had no less than thirteen according to
Aristoxenus, whose three books on the subject are
the most ancient extant. Their scales included
quarter-tones, and if they employed harmony
—which is, I believe, a somewhat contested
point—their ears could only tolerate combinations of thirds and sixths.

To the subject of ancient melody and rhythm
I may again have occasion to refer. My present
object is merely to call the reader's attention to
the fact that although the laws which regulate
the art of music have changed so much since the
time of the above-mentioned writer, who lived
in the third century before the Christian era, we

have direct evidence that many of the rules connected with the elder sister art, dancing—"the
kaleidoscope of rhythm, the prolific source whence
music has ever drawn"*—are precisely the same
to-day as they were *three thousand years ago*.
Startling as this statement may appear, it is
nevertheless a fact which can easily be verified
by an examination of some ancient mural paintings, to which I shall call attention in my next
chapter.

* ROWBOTHAM's *Hist. of Music.*

CHAPTER II.

DANCING IN ANCIENT EGYPT.

THE history of remote ages is one of those subjects about which the more we learn the less we discover that we actually know. This may appear a somewhat paradoxical remark, but it is nevertheless true. Authorities vary so widely in their statements, that when we have examined several works, and compared them, we are often forced to the conclusion that much of what we were previously disposed to accept as fact is merely a matter of speculation. As an example of this, suppose an indifferently read person were to casually open a book of ancient history and find that the date ascribed to Menes or Mena, the first - mentioned Egyptian monarch after purely mythological times, was about 2000 B.C.,* he would

---

* Date given by Samuel Sharp, who thinks the Egyptian Menes was probably Manu of the Hindoos, "their first of created beings and holiest of law-makers." If this be so, he

probably believe that he was in possession of a
fact. If, however, he extended his researches, he
would ascertain that Chabas supposes him to have
lived about 4000 B.C., while Manetho, the priest
of Heliopolis, of whose history some fragments
only remain, makes the date 5004 B.C., which is,
I believe, exactly one thousand years before the
creation of the world, according to orthodox
Biblical chronology.

But Herodotus, who has been styled "the father
of history," and by some also "the father of lies," *
tells us that from the time of Bacchus (Egyptian
Osiris) to that of Amasis are computed fifteen
thousand years ;† and Plato alludes to Egyptian
paintings executed ten thousand years before his
own time. But even these estimates of time, how-

does not appear to have entertained a very high opinion of
dancing, for he connects the representatives of the art with
"gamblers, cruel men," and other disreputable characters, and
orders their banishment from the town. It is interesting to
note that in another place this holy law-maker includes "mares,
female camels, *slave-girls*, buffalo cows, she-goats," etc., in the
same category, as if they were all creatures of precisely the
same value and importance.—Vide *Laws of Manu*, ix. 225, etc.

* De Quincey is of opinion that the honour of the latter appellation belongs rather to Suetonius, as being the inventor of
anecdotes.

† Herodotus, ii. 145.

ever extravagant they may appear to some, are quite moderate compared with those of the Chinese, who assert that as a nation they have existed for upwards of a hundred thousand years.

It is not, perhaps, to be wondered at that there should be a diversity of opinion concerning the date when the first of the Pharaohs flourished, if we consider that the whole of the seventh dynasty of kings was "historically a void," to quote the words of Sir Erasmus Wilson; and while, according to Manetho, seventy kings reigned seventy days, another authority makes the number of kings five and the period seventy years.* It seems to me that in such circumstances it would be impossible to tell even approximately when the earliest rulers of Egypt lived. Nothing is known of many of them except their names, and these are inscribed differently on the Greek and Egyptian lists. It is difficult even for expert Egyptologists to ascertain whether the early kings reigned contemporaneously or consecutively; and, so far as the supposed founder of Egyptian monarchy and builder of Memphis is concerned, not only do authorities differ with regard to the time of his

* See *Egypt of the Past.*

reign to the extent of two or three thousand years,
but some of the greatest of them consider it doubt-
ful if he ever lived at all.*

But in reading what is known of the history of
Egypt it is not the "plain, unvarnished" statements of facts, or what are supposed to be such,
that take the firmest hold on our memory, but
stories which have in them the element of romance.
For instance, who does not remember the story of
the thief who carried away the treasure of Rhamp-
sinitus; of the maiden entombed in a golden cow;†
of the beautiful flaxen-haired Nitocris, who prepared a sumptuous entertainment in a subterranean
hall for the men who had murdered her brother,
and who drowned them as they feasted by letting
in the waters of the Nile ? We remember Proteus
because of the fabulous stories‡ concerning his

---

* "He must be ranked amongst those founders of monarchies
whose personal existence a severe and enlightened criticism
doubts or denies."—Dr. BIRCH, _Ancient Egypt_.

† The daughter of Mycerinus.

‡ Supposed to be the Memnon of the Sighing Statue. Sir G.
Wilkinson thinks that the fiction probably arose from his frequent changes of headdress, but Lucian is of opinion that it
signified nothing more than that he was a very expert dancer,
who had a particular talent for pantomime, and could, in a
manner, turn himself into anything.

C

ability to change his form; the name of Cheops is familiar on account of his cruel oppression of the people and scandalous conduct, if we may trust the statement of Herodotus, and because of the mighty pyramid which bears his name. Beyond these a few monarchs, like the third Thothmes and the great Rameses or Sesostris, stand out conspicuously among long lists of rulers of whom scarcely anything is recorded.

However, if we are not fortunate enough to possess any reliable information concerning the chronology of the ancient Egyptians, and if we know very little of their history, we are at least able to form, what is far more to our present purpose, a fairly accurate conception of their manners and customs. Of their dances and manner of dancing it is indeed surprising that so much is known, when we consider that their chief books are of a distinctly religious and by no means festive character. It is not to be expected that we should learn much about dancing from such lugubrious productions as the *Ritual or Book of the Dead* * and the *Book of Lamentations or Sighs of Isis,*

* Quotations beginning "I am yesterday," etc., may be found in RAWLINSON'S *Ancient Egypt*, chap. v.

from *Hymns to the gods* or *Treatises on Mathematics*.* Even the paintings and sculptures, from which we derive so largely our ideas of Egyptian social life, have been found principally in the tombs of kings. But, notwithstanding the sepulchral nature of these productions, they afford abundant evidence that the ancient Egyptians, among other accomplishments, knew not only how to dance, but how to dance well.

The classic writers of Greece and Rome speak incidentally of Egyptian dances, but I have not found that they give many particulars concerning them. The historian of Halicarnassus, though he enters into strangely minute details concerning the habits and peculiarities of the people, does not, so far as I can remember, allude to their manner of dancing. True, he mentions the song called by them "Maneros," which was probably accompanied by bodily movements, and says it is the same as the Greek "Linus," which was sung in memory of Urania's handsome son, whom Apollo slew because he boasted himself equal to a god. Herodotus conjectures as to whence the Egyptians could have got

* For translations of works, including novelettes, see *Records of the Past*.

this music, and says they assured him that Maneros
was the only son of the first king of Egypt, and that,
happening to die prematurely, he was honoured by
the Egyptians with this funeral dirge.* Pausanias
states that "on the death of Linus sorrow for him
spread even to foreign lands, so that even Egypt has
a lament called 'Linus,' but in their own dialect
'Maneros.'" †

Of these ancient writers we know that the former
has been accused of excessive partiality for his own
country,‡ and Pausanias would naturally incline to
favour the country in which he travelled; but as
Herodotus admits that the Egyptians "seem to
have sung the 'Maneros' from time immemorial,"
and since, according to Plato, the Greeks were
regarded by the Egyptians as mere children compared with them in point of antiquity,§ I am of
opinion that, as the same music was sung in both
countries, it is more than probable that the Greeks
borrowed it from the Egyptians.

Certainly it was from Egypt that the Greeks and

---

* Herodotus, ii. 79.
† *Description of Greece*, book ix., chap. xxix.
‡ DISRAELI, *Sketches of Criticism*.
§ Plato in *Tim.*, p. 467.

Romans borrowed their dance of the chief mimic at the funerals of important personages. A man skilled in imitating the personal idiosyncrasies and manners of others was appointed by the relatives of the deceased to enact the part, and dressed in the dead man's garments, and having his face covered with a mask as nearly as possible resembling the face of the deceased, the dancer immediately preceded the hearse,* and as the procession moved slowly along to the sound of solemn music, probably the "Linus," he performed a pantomimic dance, representing by his actions all the most remarkable deeds achieved during his lifetime by the man who was being carried to his tomb. I was almost saying to his last resting-place ; but that expression would have been inaccurate, since the mummies of so many great Egyptians have been removed to adorn the British and other European museums.

It is not surprising that, in a country which we are accustomed to associate with ideas of all that is vast and magnificent in conception and design, there should have originated what may perhaps be termed

* A peculiar kind of four-wheeled hearse is represented in Sir G. WILKINSON's *Manners and Customs of the Ancient Egyptians,* plate 69.

the sublimest of all dances. This was the Astronomic Dance, in which, by regulated figures, steps,
and movements, the order and harmonious motion
of the celestial bodies was represented to the music
of the flute, lyre, and syrinx. This dance was
clearly connected with the worship of the sun, *Ra*,
with whom, at a later period, all the principal
deities were more or less closely connected.* It
was performed by the Greeks around the blazing
altar of Jupiter. It was associated with the rites
of Dionysus (Bacchus), who was the Greek representative of Osiris, the Egyptian deity most
generally worshipped, and also of Baal Peor, the
Semitic sun-god.† But the Bacchic Dithyramb was,
I should imagine, a very corrupt form of the Astronomic Dance; indeed, previous to the salutary
reformation effected by Arion it could have been
little better than a drunken orgie of the most
dissolute character. The Astronomic Dance was
also performed on the stage, not, of course, by the
Egyptians—for they had no theatre—but by the
Greeks, among whom it was held in high estimation.

* Dr. BIRCH, *Ancient Egypt*, Introduction; RAWLINSON'S *Hist.*,
p. 354.

† Dr. DONALDSON, *Theatre of the Greeks.*

Plato and other philosophers allude to this dance as
"a divine institution."

All dancing was originally more or less closely
connected with religion, but it seems to have been
not unfrequently practised by the ancient Egyptians
for purely recreative purposes, both by men and
women, sometimes together and sometimes separately. In the case of hired dancers, females were
generally preferred, probably on account of their
superior elegance. A refined style of dancing, consisting of graceful attitudes and dignified movements, seems to have been best appreciated and
most frequently performed at the entertainments of
the rich, and before spectators of exalted rank, who
would, as might be expected, naturally evince the
most cultivated taste—an expectation, by the way,
which is not always realised in such matters at the
present time. Among the lower classes grotesque
dances were more in favour, and these sometimes
degenerated into the merest buffoonery ; indeed,
hired dancers varied the character of their movements according to the tastes and social status of
those by whom they were employed.

The dances at entertainments were always performed to the sound of music, and frequently appear

to have been accompanied by the clapping of
hands. The instruments chiefly employed were
the Egyptian guitar, used both by men and women,
the single and double pipe, the harp, lyre, and
flute, the latter being used generally by men.
Sometimes the musicians danced while they played.
Wilkinson has a drawing (Plate 247) representing
a girl executing not ungracefully a forward movement while playing on the guitar, and another
(Plate 253) of a woman simultaneously dancing
and playing the double pipe.

The dresses worn by professional dancing girls
at entertainments were extremely simple. A loose
robe of the flimsiest possible material, reaching from
the shoulders to the ankles, completed their attire.
Sometimes the dress was fastened at the waist by a
kestos, or girdle, but generally it was permitted to
flow freely, and judging from the paintings, the
texture must have been so fine as to have allowed
the movements of the limbs to show plainly
beneath. In some cases the female dancers are
represented entirely nude. There is in the Egyptian
gallery of the British Museum a wall painting taken
from a tomb at Thebes. It is situated, if my
memory does not fail me, about midway up the

room on the right-hand side as you face the colossal
statue of Thothmes. The painting is supposed to
have been executed during the eighteenth or nine-
teenth dynasty, and in it are two dancing girls
facing opposite directions. There is plenty of action
depicted in these figures. In one the hands are
raised high above the head; in the other they are
lowered. One female not dancing is represented
playing a double pipe, and others are clapping
their hands. The accompanists are dressed, but
the dancers wear only a *kestos*.

I read that professional dancers are represented
thus in paintings which I have not myself had
the opportunity of seeing, and also it is stated
that the accessories leave no room for doubt that
the entertainments were given by people of the
highest respectability.

Sir Gardner Wilkinson is of opinion that the
outline of the transparent robe worn by these
girls may, in some instances, have been accidentally
effaced;* but Dr. Birch says "it is certain they
sometimes danced naked, as their successors, the
Alméhs, do." We read in the latter writer's introduction to *Egypt from the Earliest Times* that

* *Manners and Customs*, chap. vi.

the children went entirely undressed till they
arrived at the age of puberty, and Professor Rawlinson thinks that, owing to this custom, the nudity
of the dancing girls might seem less strange and
indelicate.* *Tempora mutantur;* but even at the
present day, in what is somewhat anomalously
termed full dress, the bodies of female dancers
do not in some cases appear overburdened with
apparel, and not very long since a kind of dance
was introduced on the stage in which the costume
of the performer was so arranged that the spectators caught occasional glimpses of her figure
in an apparently nude condition amidst a cloud
of gauzy drapery. The nature of this dance and
its accessories have since been considerably modified, but it shows how little appreciation there can
be for true art when dancers are obliged to have
recourse to such expedients to attract public
attention.

Returning, however, to the Egyptians, of social
dancing among them it is almost impossible, I
think, to speak with any degree of certainty.
Wilkinson tells us that "it was not customary for
the upper orders to indulge in this amusement

* *Hist. Ancient Egypt,* p. 549.

either in public or private, and none appear to have practised it but the lower ranks of society and those who gained their livelihood by attending festive meetings." Further on he states that the reason the Egyptians forbade those of the higher classes to learn dancing as an accomplishment, or even as an amusement, was because "they dreaded the excitement resulting from such an occupation, the excess of which ruffled and discomposed the mind"; and "it would have been difficult," continues Wilkinson, "having once conceded permission to indulge in it, to prevent excesses which it did not require the example of Asiatic nations to teach them to foresee."

But were the Egyptian ladies really forbidden to practise dancing? We know that the Greeks did not consider it beneath the dignity of persons of the highest rank to dance, neither did the Hebrews, who, as I think is generally admitted, derived their dances from the Egyptians. It is not at all likely that the Israelites would have remained in a land for upwards of four hundred years[*] without becoming imbued with the customs,

* Wilkinson supposes the pacific Pharaoh of Joseph's time to have been Usertesen I., of the sixteenth dynasty, and the

notions, and even prejudices of the people among
whom they dwelt, and with whom they were, for a
time at least, on amicable terms. Yet we read
that no sooner had they safely accomplished the
passage across the Red Sea than Miriam, the sister
of Moses and Aaron, and herself a prophetess,
took a timbrel or tambourine in her hand, and
danced with other women to celebrate the over-
throw of their late taskmasters.*

There are, of course, other notable instances in
the Bible which tend to show that among the
Jews it was customary for people of the most
exalted rank to dance. Some of these will be
alluded to in due course, but I now mention the
circumstance of Miriam's dancing because it occurred immediately the Israelites had left a land
where we are told that dancing was only taught
as an accomplishment to slaves and people of the
lower orders. That the Jews were actually strongly
influenced by Egyptian customs and superstitions
we have abundant evidence to show; but here it
will be sufficient to mention two instances, the em-

Pharaoh of Exodus the warlike Thothmes III., of the eighteenth
dynasty.

* Exod. xv.

balming of Joseph and the dance around the golden
calf in the wilderness, which was simply an imitation of the worship of Apis. I observe that in a
paragraph contributed by him to Sir G. Wilkinson's *Ancient Egyptians* Dr. Birch expresses the
conviction that, although the ballet was not in use
among them, there is reason to believe that dances,
" representing a continuous action or argument of
a story," were in use privately ; and he states that
such dances were executed " by ladies and other
persons attached to the harem or household," as
well as by hired performers. In another passage
Dr. Birch alludes to a representation in the tomb
of Anmut, of the sixth dynasty, of a dance by
four ladies of the harem, and in the Introduction
to his small history he merely mentions that the
Egyptian women danced, without making any reference to social distinction in connection with
the subject.

On the whole, I think we may not unreasonably
infer that, although in the mural paintings most
of the people represented as dancing appear to
have been professional performers, it is quite
probable that dancing was also practised privately
as an amusement by Egyptians of the upper classes,

though certainly the art was not cultivated or
nearly so highly esteemed by them as it was by
the aristocracy of ancient Greece.

At the same time, there exist sculptures which,
as previously stated, go to show that Egyptians
of the superior order were by no means wanting
in appreciation of true gracefulness, either of gesture
or action. Some of these are reproduced in **Wilkin-**
son's magnificent work to which I have already so
frequently referred. Notably there is one of the
time of Amenophis II. from one of the oldest
tombs at Thebes (about 1450 B.C.). The woodcut
is marked 261, and the original from which it was
taken appears to be somewhat dilapidated; but
allowing for this, and also for the very imperfect
condition of Egyptian pictorial art, the work is
by no means discreditable, and the attitudes assumed by the dancers appear to have been graceful
enough. Four women are represented as playing
and dancing at the same time, but their instruments are for the most part obliterated. A fifth
figure is resting on one knee, with her hands crossed
before her breast. The posing of the heads in
these figures is generally good. In another painting from Beni Hassan, executed about three thou-

sand five hundred years ago—one of those to which allusion was made in my last chapter—a dancer is represented in the act of performing a pirouette* in the extended fourth position. The arms are fully outstretched, and the general attitude of the figure is precisely as it might be in executing a similar movement at the present day. It is also noticeable that the angle formed by the upper part of the foot and fore part of the leg is very obtuse, which is quite in accordance with artistic rules, while the natural inclination of an inexperienced and untrained dancer when holding the limb in such a position would be to bend the foot towards the shin, or at least to keep it in its normal position at right angles.

From these and many other paintings and sculptures that have been discovered we may gather that the primary rules by which the movements of dancers are governed *have not altered appreciably during three thousand and odd years.* The first thing the Egyptian dancers were taught was evidently to turn their toes outward and downward, and special attention was paid to the positions of

* Erroneously supposed to have been an invention of the later Italian school.

their arms, which were frequently gracefully extended, and also raised high, with the hands almost
joining above the head.

In the small tablet of Baken-Amen representing
the adoration of Osiris, now in the British Museum,
some of the arm positions of the figures are very
good, although in this instance they are not supposed to be dancing. In one of the sculptures
from Thebes, of which I have seen an illustration,
a figure is unmistakably performing an *entrechat*.
The Egyptian dancers frequently employed *jettés*,
coupés, *cabrioles*, and toe-and-heel movements. In
Wilkinson's *Ancient Egyptians* there is a plate
representing dance figures for two performers, from
Upper and Lower Egypt, some of which are also
engraved in other works. They form apparently
a kind of minuet. Between the dancers in each
figure are inscriptions which, we are informed,
refer to the name thereof. Thus, for instance, one
was called "*mek terf mas*," or "making the figure
of the calf"; another was "*mek terf nub ti*," or
"making the figure of taking gold"; and a third
was "*mek wa snut*," or "making a pirouette." The
last-mentioned appears, from the picture, to have
been a movement in which the dancers turned

each other under the arms, as in the *pas d'Alle-mande.*

Athor was supposed by the ancient Egyptians to preside over the choric art. She is styled the "celestial mother" and "lady of the dance and mirth." This goddess has been identified by the Greeks with their Aphrodite, and by the Romans with their Venus.

D

CHAPTER III.

DANCES OF THE GREEKS.

READERS who are accustomed to regard dancing merely as an evening recreation, or as a light accomplishment cultivated chiefly by professional artistes, will scarcely be able to realise the important part it played not only in the daily life, but in the religious observances, warlike training of youths, and general education, of the ancient Greeks.*

If we desire to form a just conception of the nature of Greek dances, it will be necessary to bear in mind the fact that in many respects the manners, customs, and even morals of those who performed them were totally different from our own. The observation previously made, that the primary rules

* Mr. Walter Pater observes : " . . . Their education, which indeed makes no sharp distinction between mental and bodily exercise, results, as it had begun, in ' music '—ends with the body, mind, memory above all, at their finest—on great show-days in the dance. —" Lacedæmon," *Contemporary Review*, June, 1892.

34

by which the movements of dancers are governed
have not changed appreciably during three thousand
years, applies only to the actions of the limbs, and
not to the nature or accessories of the dance
performed.

In reading the works of ancient writers, and in
visiting the ruins of ancient cities, we are continually reminded of the vast difference which
exists between our own conceptions of what is
proper and becoming, and those by which the men
and women of past ages were influenced. Many
choric performances, that in Athens and Sparta
were considered perfectly consistent with gravity
and decorum, would, if performed in modern London,
appear either excessively ludicrous or grossly improper. We can scarcely, for instance, conceive the
spectacle of a great poet of our own times acting as
choryphæus to a band of tipsy revellers; yet one
of the most ancient poets of Greece, Archilochus,
makes a positive boast of the fact that he " knows
how to lead the Dithyramb with the thunder of
wine upon his mind." * Again, what should we
have thought if, during the Zulu or Egyptian wars,
on receiving the news of some battle gained, our

* GROTE'S *Hist.*, chap. xxix., quoted also by Dr. Donaldson.

greatest dramatic writer had divested himself of his
garments and, after being anointed with oil, had
danced thus publicly around a trophy erected on
the occasion to the music of a lyre? Yet this is
precisely what Sophocles did after the victory of
Salamis.* It is not related if he, like the older
poet already mentioned, had also the "thunder of
wine upon his mind." Presumably he was quite in
his sober senses, for he appears to have been far
more abstemious than the other Greek poets, and is
said to have reprimanded Æschylus with imbibing
too freely, accusing him of not being aware "that
he was doing right even when such was the case."†

I merely mention these instances because I wish
to point out that we must not judge of the propriety
of Greek dances by modern standards or tastes. The
Dithyramb was a dance which, from its very nature
and the fact of its having been instituted in honour
of Dionysus, or Bacchus, was intimately connected
with the element of intoxication. A condition of
strong mental excitement on the part of the dancers
generally, and especially of their leader, seems to

* This is related by Athenæus, who adds, however, "Some say
he had his tunic on."

† Chamaeleon in Athenæus, book i., xxxix.

have been indispensable for its successful performance. We are told by Epicharmus that "there is
no Dithyramb if you drink water,"* and from Lucian
and many other writers we may infer that it was
considered quite out of order—quite "bad form"—
to dance it in a state of sobriety.

The Dithyramb was, it is true, admittedly a dance
of loose character, but the same cannot be said of
the Pyrrhic and Gymnopædic dances, which were
considered among the most noble and praiseworthy
ever introduced by the ancients. Yet even in these
it was customary not only for youths to dance
entirely without clothes, but sometimes the maidens
were permitted to join them also in that state of
nature which, as the translator of Noverre admirably
says in his preface, "our degeneracy alone has made
a reproach."

We must always remember that the religion of
the Greeks consisted in the deification of the various
powers of nature, and, such being the case, they
could discover no harm in many things which to us
may appear disgraceful.† In some respects they

---

* Quoted by Dr. Donaldson in *Theatre of the Greeks*.

† In Lucian's tract of the Syrian goddess Dionysus is represented as testifying his regard for his stepmother in what would
appear to us a very curious manner.

were more innocent than we, in fact more like
children, and doubtless Athenæus was perfectly
sincere when he spoke of a certain fashion in Sparta
as being much praised, and exclaimed that it was a
beautiful sight to behold the young men and
maidens wrestling thus together.* Lycurgus ex-
plained that the practice of admitting the Spartan
girls to these dances and exercises was introduced
so that they should not grow up inferior to the
young men in bodily strength and vigour.†

Among the ancient Greeks the culture of physical
grace and beauty was considered of paramount
importance. It was in fact a part of their religion.
We read in the *Dialogue of Charidemus*, attributed
to Lucian, that the heavens and earth, mortals and
immortal gods, unanimously proclaim beauty "the
most excellent of all things." And they perceived
that clumsiness of movement, pose, or gesture
detracts from the effect of personal loveliness, however perfect it may appear, while beauty of form
and feature is always enhanced by grace of move-

---

* *Deipnosophists,* book xiii. 20.

† Dr. Donaldson (*Greek Theatre*) says that the γυμνοπαιδια, or
"festival of naked youths," was held in great esteem at Sparta,
and was considered a sort of introduction to the Pyrrhic. See
also Pausanias, book iii , chap. ix.

ment.* And, perceiving this, they set themselves
to invent dances by the practice of which gracefulness might be developed. Such, for instance, must
have been the Dance of Innocence, which Helen of
Sparta was practising as a little girl in the temple
of Artemis when she was surprised and carried
away by Theseus, who, according to Plutarch, must
have been fifty years old at the time,† old enough,
indeed, to have known better than to act thus. But
it is only fair to the memory of the hero to mention
that, according to a tradition related by Pausanias,‡
Helen must have been considerably more than ten
years of age when Theseus eloped with her. The
translator of Noverre's letters points out how some
ill-natured writers aver that, pleased with her first
elopement, at her return she frequently paid homage
to Diana, and that it was from the temple, and not
from her husband's house, that she was abducted
for the second time in her life by Paris. I find
that, according to some authorities, the Queen of
Sparta was at this period by no means a child, having

* Lucian in his *Ship, or, The Wishes*, speaks of the girls of
Athens as being "practised in graceful attitudes."

† *Life of Theseus.*

‡ *Description of Greece*, book ii. chap. xxii.

in fact already passed the age which Balsac considered the most charming in woman by some
twenty years. If this be correct, at the time when
Troy was reduced to ashes she must have been
tolerably well advanced in life — a condition of
things which ill assimilates with the glowing
descriptions of her incomparable beauty in the
Iliad. But perhaps, owing to the miraculous in-
cidents of her birth and parentage, she was not
destined to wither as ordinary mortals, but, like
a later heroine, Ninon de l'Enclos, continued to
flourish in perennial youth.*

It is not, however, with the after-life of the
young votary of Artemis that we are here concerned, but with the nature of her dance. It was,
we are told, performed by young maidens before
the altar of the goddess, and consisted of grave
steps and graceful, modest attitudes belonging to
that order of choric movement called by the Greeks
ἐμμέλεια, or *emmeleia* in more familiar characters.
This was the general term employed to express

* In the fifteenth book of the *Odyssey* Homer still speaks of
Helen as " fair-haired " and " fair-cheeked," although the commencement of the fourth book seems to show that she was in
advanced life when she returned to Menelaus.

the noble and serious style of dancing, the most
solemn forms of gymnopædic gesticulation.* It
was the dance of tragedy, and all its movements
were dignified and stately.

The style of dance most directly opposed to this
was the comic, called κορδαξ, or *cordax*, which,
according to all accounts, does not appear to have
been renowned for its respectability. Athenæus
speaks of it as being, among the Greeks, an "inde-
corous dance"; Lucian says it was considered a
shame to dance it when sober; and Aristophanes
claims credit for its omission in the *Clouds*.†

These were the two extremes of dancing, corre-
sponding—if any comparison can fairly be made—
to our serious and grotesque styles, though all the
dances included under the head of *cordax* were
not necessarily grotesque, some being merely lively.
A kind of dance that partook partly of the nature
of each of those mentioned in the preceding paragraphs, but consisted chiefly of vigorous movements, was called σικιννις, or *sicinnis*, bearing,
perhaps, some resemblance to what we term
demi - caractère. These three orders of dancing

* DONALDSON'S *Greek Theatre*, p. 267.
† *Ibid.*

belonged more especially, perhaps, to dramatic
representation. Lucian tells us that they received
their names from three Satyrs in the retinue of
Dionysus, who are reported to have been their
inventors; but Athenæus states that the last-
mentioned was the invention of a barbarian
named Sicinnus.*

Concerning the practice of dancing in the Heroic
Age, we are able to glean some information from
the pages of Homer. In these early days dancing
appears to have been held in the highest esteem
as a domestic pastime; and that it was originally
entirely disassociated from those questionable
features which seem, unfortunately, to have been
the product of a more advanced civilisation, we
may infer from the fact that in the thirteenth
book of the *Iliad* we find the epithet "blameless"
or "harmless" applied to the dance, which is included among those sweet and agreeable pleasures
"with which one would much more readily satisfy
his desire than with war."

In the Homeric hymn to Apollo we read how

---

* In another place Athenæus says that the word was practically
formed from κινησις, meaning motion, because in dancing it the
Satyrs used the most rapid movements.

the Ionians, "with their children and respected
wives," were accustomed to assemble in honour
of the god, and delight him with their boxing,
singing, and dancing. The words of the poet go
to show that dancing was at that time an amusement or art in which everybody could join, and
that it was by no means cultivated only by professional artistes. The Ionians seem to have been
always renowned for their love of dancing, but
unfortunately their dances degenerated in character so greatly in later years that certain specially
wanton and voluptuous gesticulations came to be
known by the Romans as "Ionic movements."

In another part of the same hymn Homer represents the immortals themselves as sporting in the
dance: "The fair-haired Graces, the wise Hours
and Harmony, and Hebe, and Venus, the daughter
of Jove, dance, holding each other's hands by the
wrist." They dance to music played by the chaste
Diana, and are joined by Mercury and Mars.
Then Phœbus Apollo himself "strikes the harp,
taking grand and lofty steps, and a shining haze
surrounds him, and glittering of feet and of his
well-fitted tunic." It appears also that this display of choric talent on the part of Phœbus is a

special source of delight to his illustrious parents,
"the golden-tressed Latona and deep-scheming Jove."

Another conspicuous figure in ancient mythology,
Pan, who was numbered among the greater gods by
the Egyptians as well as by the Greeks, is represented by Homer as "going hither and thither in
the midst of the dancers, moving rapidly with his
feet." But judging from the form in which this
deity is usually represented—a form from which
mediæval artists took their crude ideas of a certain
unmentionable personage—his efforts in dancing
must have been singularly devoid of elegance; and
perhaps if Diana had beheld them she would not
have been so easily tempted to forget her obliga-
tions on his account.

Now, seeing that the gods themselves, and gods
of the first order, too—the "smartest set" in
Olympus—were supposed to take pleasure in the
dance, and, with the exception of Pan, were, as
a matter of course, accomplished dancers, it is
not to be wondered at that the greatest respect
was entertained for this art by the ancient Greeks,
and that it should have formed an indispensable
accessory in their public worship, just as the sister
art, music, does with us.

There were Christians of early times who believed that the angels danced in heaven, as even
the most orthodox still believe they sing; and,
believing this, they introduced dancing in the
choirs of churches. But although, as I shall elsewhere point out, attempts have, from time to time,
been made to revive the practice, it has never, since
its abolishment in consequence of the scandals
connected with the Agapæ, again obtained a permanent place in the ceremonial of religion.

Our conceptions of dancing, and the practice
thereof, have so changed during the later centuries,
and it has become so intimately associated in our
minds with worldly festivity, and even frivolity,
that it seems almost irreverent to speak of dancing
in connection with religion. But if we consider
the matter critically, and from a purely impartial
standpoint, the employment of solemn, and even
livelier, movements and gestures, does not appear
an inconsistent manner of paying adoration to the
Deity, especially when we remember the words of
the Psalmist, " Let us praise His name in the dance;
let us sing praises unto Him with the timbrel and
harp."*

* Psalm cxlix. 3.

Doubtless the kind of dancing which the ancients connected with religious worship bore a distinct character, and differed from the dancing that was performed for mere amusement, just as the style of music that we term sacred differs from that which we term secular. The distinction does not at all depend upon the sadness or joyfulness of the melodies, but rather on their construction, the manner in which they are harmonised, and the nature of the cadences. And so, I conclude, it must have been with the dances which the Greeks held in honour of their gods. They may have been refined, or boisterous, or obscene, according to the nature of the deity worshipped, but certainly they were altogether different from those dances which were purely domestic.

The nature of the Greek religion was such that many of their sacred dances would, according to our notions, be far less reputable than those which were simply social. Any student of mythology or ancient history, into whose hands these pages may chance to fall, will understand the purport of these remarks; but for the general reader it will be sufficient to point out that while on the one hand the dances connected with the rites of Dionysus* or Priapus were necessarily of a shameless and degraded nature, on the other hand those which were instituted in honour of Apollo, the Pæans of Lacedæmon, Crete, and Delos, were eminently dignified and noble.

Scheigel, in his general survey of the drama, expresses the opinion that the nature worship "which fancy among other nations darkened with hideous shapes, hardening the heart to cruelty," assumed among the Greeks "a form of grandeur, dignity, and mildness." Nevertheless it is a fact that they did occasionally offer up human victims. In Beotia a beautiful boy was sacrificed yearly to Dionysus, until eventually a kid was substituted for the victim;† and the Ionians who dwelt in Aroe, Anthea, and Mesatis, offered up an annual

* There appears to have been considerable opposition to the establishment of Bacchic worship in Greece. Henry Riley, in his explanation of the first fable in the fourth book of Ovid's *Metamorphosis*, points out how it was probably published by the priests among other "miracles and prodigies" the more easily to influence the minds of their fellow-men. Thus the daughters of Minyas are said to have been changed into bats solely because they neglected to join in the orgies of that god (Bacchus, or Dionysus), when probably the fact was that they were either secretly despatched, or were forced to fly for their lives. See also fable of Pentheus, 8, book iii., and *Bacchantes* of Euripides.

† DONALDSON's *Greek Theatre*.

sacrifice in the shape of the loveliest youth and
maiden that could be found in the country, to
satisfy the revenge of Artemis for the offence of
Melanippus and Comætho.* We also learn from
Plutarch† and other writers with what great
severity the Helots were treated by their Spartan
conquerors. Still I daresay by comparison with
the barbarous customs of surrounding nations, the
atrocious cruelties they practised, and the hideous
nature of some of their religious rites,‡ the institutions and general character of the ancient Greeks
might, on the whole, be considered humane.

That dancing was highly esteemed as an accomplishment for young ladies in the Heroic Age we
may gather from the fact that gentle, " white-armed
Nausicaa," the daughter of a king, is represented as
leading her companions in " the choral lay" after
they have washed their linen in the stream, and
amused themselves awhile with a game at ball.
And Ulysses compliments her specially upon her
choric skill ; for, after artfully pretending that he is
by no means certain whether she may not be a

* PAUSANIAS, *Greece*, book vii., chap. xix.
† *Life of Lycurgus.*
‡ *c.g.*, rites of Baal, Moloch, etc.

goddess, even Diana, daughter of the mighty Jove,
he adds that, if she should chance to be "one of
those mortals who dwell on earth," he feels sure
that the minds of her "thrice-blessed sire, brother,
and venerable mother" must be ever delighted when
they behold her "entering the dance."

The above episode occurs in the sixth book of
the *Odyssey*. In the eighth book we read how
Ulysses was entertained at the court of Alcinous,
the father of the young lady who had befriended
him, and whose dancing he had so greatly admired.
Here again the astonishment and admiration of the
wanderer were excited by the rapid and skilful
movements of the dancers, who now were not
maidens only, but "youths in the prime of life."
Presently two of the most accomplished among
them, Halius and Laodamus by name, were selected
by Alcinous to exhibit their skill in a dance, during
which one performer threw a ball high up in the
air, while the other caught it between his feet
before it reached the ground. From the lines which
follow, it appears that this was a true dance, not a
mere acrobatic performance, and that the purple
ball was simply used as an accessory, just as a
skipping-rope is sometimes used by us.

E

From the twenty-third book of the same poem we
may infer that dancing among the guests at wedding
festivals formed in these early times an essential
part of the ceremonies.*   The wanderer, having at
length been recognised by the faithful Penelope, tells
his son, Telemachus, to "let the divine bard who
has the tuneful harp lead the sportful dance, so that
anyone hearing it from without may say it is a
marriage." Here again the poet applies the epithet
"harmless" to the dance, telling us how those
assembled made themselves ready to join therein,
and how "the great house resounded with the feet
of men and beautiful girded women making merry."

In commencing to describe the various scenes
which Vulcan wrought on the shield of Achilles,
Homer also associates dancing with hymeneal festivities.   "In one indeed there were marriages and
feasts; and they were conducting the brides to their
chambers through the city with brilliant torches,
and many a bridal song was raised," and youthful
dancers were "wheeling round" to the music of the
pipe and lyre.   Another design with which the
lame god adorned this famous shield represented
the dance "contrived by Dædalus for fair-haired

* See also SMITH's *Antiquities.*

Ariadne." In this dance youths with tunics and "golden swords" suspended from "silver belts" and virgins clothed in fine linen robes, and wearing "beautiful garlands," danced together, "holding each other's hands by the wrists." * And they danced in a circle, "bounding nimbly with skilled feet, as when a potter, sitting, shall make trial of a wheel fitted to his hands, whether it will run; and at other times again they ran back to their places through one another."

A dance of a similar nature to the above was performed together by the youths and maidens of Lacedæmon. It was called by them ὅρμος (hormos), or the Necklace, and is described by Lucian, who tells us how it was commenced by a youth, who led the dance and performed steps of a military nature, such as he was afterwards to march in the field. Then followed a maiden, who, leading up her companions, danced in a gentle and graceful manner, as was becoming to her sex. Thus, we are told, "the whole formed a chain of masculine vigour and feminine modesty entwined together." † This dance

---

* Mr. Gladstone alludes to this passage in *Juventus Mundi*, pp. 403-4.

† Dialogue *de saltatione* between Lycinus and Crato.

is said also to have been similar to the dance performed at the gymnopædia, to which allusion has
already been made, and which, together with the
Pyrrhic and Hyporchematic dances, hereafter to be
described, developed originally from the Pæan.*

In the comedies of Aristophanes frequent mention
is made of dances which appear to have been
executed in a ring. Thus in the *Thesmophoriazusæ* :
" Put yourself in motion, each of you; advance; come
lightly with your feet in a circle; join hand to hand;
move to the time of the dance ; go with swift feet.
It behoveth the choral order to look about, turning
the eye in every direction." In the *Frogs* both
Xanthias and Bacchus express a strong desire to
dance with a young girl whom they appear to have
been observing somewhat too intently. The dance
in this comedy is performed by the initiated in
honour of Iacchus, and forms "a humorous representation of the concluding ceremony of the Eleusinian
mysteries, on the last day of which the worship of
Bacchus, under the invocation of Iacchus, was
united with that of Ceres." †

Although, as a comic dramatist, Aristophanes was

* *Vide* DONALDSON'S *Greek Theatre.*
† FRERE.

doubtless greatly admired in his own day, there is
not much in those of his comedies which have
been preserved that would bear quotation in these
pages, especially in the *Lysistrata*. It happens,
however, that this play ends with a poetic description of a very beautiful Laconian dance called the
Dipodia, a dance which those elegant female figures
that we so frequently find represented on ancient
bas-reliefs, with their heads crowned with reeds
and their hands raised above them, are supposed to
be executing.*

From the comedy it would appear that both men
and women joined in the dance, for Lysistrata
herself, exhorting the Spartans to lead away the
women, says, "Let husband stand beside wife, and
wife beside husband; and then, having danced in
honour of the gods for our good fortune, let us
be cautious henceforth to sin no more." Finally
the chorus invokes the Spartan muse to come from
lovely Taygetus and celebrate Apollo, Minerva, and
the brave Tyndaridæ, who sport beside the Eurotas.
"Come hither," they sing, "to celebrate Sparta,
where there are choruses in honour of the gods and
the noise of dancing, where, like young horses, the

* FOSBROKE'S *Antiquities* and MÜLLER'S *Dorians*.

maidens on the banks of the Eurotas move rapidly their feet, and their tresses are agitated like those of bacchanals, brandishing the thyrsus and sporting, and the chaste daughter of Leda, the lovely leader of the chorus, directs them. Now come, bind up your hair, and leap like fawns; now strike the measured tune which cheers the chorus!"

Such, then, was the animated Dipodia, and graceful indeed must have appeared the movements of the Lacedæmonian maidens, unrestrained as they were by any of those inartistic tight-fitting or abnormally protruding garments such as are now sometimes designed, apparently to distort the human form out of all natural shape. The simple flowing chitons which they wore flowed freely with the movements of their limbs, or fell in naturally graceful lines appropriate to the postures they assumed.

Another dance, in which the Spartan girls frequently displayed their wonderful agility, was called the Bibasis ($Bιβασις$). It was also practised by men, but in a verse preserved by Pollux mention is made of a Laconian maiden who greatly excelled in the Bibasis, and had indeed danced it a thousand times more than any other girl had done.* The

* This verse is mentioned both by Smith and Müller.

great art in performing this dance was, it appears,
to spring upward from the ground and perform a
cabriole en arrière, striking the feet together behind
before alighting. A *jetté* probably was added, and
the upward springs made first from one foot and
then from the other, since it would be neither
graceful nor pleasing to keep jumping from both
feet and striking the heels behind. Anyhow the
number of successful strokes was counted, and the
most skilful performer received a prize. The women
of the chorus in Aristophanes presumably refer to
the Bibasis when they sing, " For I would never be
tired with dancing, nor would exhausting weariness
seize my knees." *

In one of Fielding's novels the author relates that
the profession of a dancing-master is one for which
he has always entertained the greatest respect ; and
he is not joking, as some ill-natured readers might
imagine. Henry Fielding was a man who had read
much, and he knew that not a few of the greatest
geniuses that ever figured in the world's history had
either taught or practised the art of dancing. Even
in Fielding's time dancing was a far more serious
matter than it is now. Graceful hand-to-hand

* *Lysistrata.*

dances were the order of the day, and people did
not then spend the whole evening whirling around
one another. But the novelist knew, doubtless, that
among the dancing-masters of ancient times must be
included the names of Thespis, Pratinas, Carcinus,
and Phrynichus, who "were called dancing poets,
because they not only made their dramas depend
upon the dancing of the chorus, but because, besides
directing the exhibition of their own plays, they
also *taught dancing to all who wished to learn.*" *
The immortal Æschylus, who is frequently styled
the " father of tragedy," was not only a great
improver of the art of dancing and the inventor of
many new figures, but was himself a teacher thereof.
Sophocles, as we have already seen, was a dancer
and musician, and he is reported to have been
highly accomplished in both arts, having received
instruction when a boy from the celebrated Lamprus.
Arion, an earlier poet than any of those mentioned
in the present paragraph, was also distinguished for
his musical and terpsichorean talent, and for having,
greatly to his credit, converted the shameless Dithyramb into a comparatively respectable dance, which
he caused to be performed by a chorus of fifty well-

* ATHENÆUS, *Deipnosophists*, book i. 39.

trained and orderly dancers around the blazing altar
of the god.*

It is said by Athenæus, Lucian, and others that
Socrates frequently diverted himself by dancing,
that he thought very highly of the art, and enjoyed
being a spectator to the clever performances of other
dancers.† It is evident also from his *Republic* and
Laws that Plato must have thoroughly understood
the rules by which the art was governed, that he
must have considered it an indispensable branch of
education, and appreciated it as a desirable social
accomplishment for young people. ‡ Moreover, he
is said to have himself "performed cyclean dances
with a ballet of boys."

But it is not necessary to go on multiplying
instances of great geniuses whose names are associated with dancing, since nearly all the ancient
writers have something to say on the subject, and
among the Greeks it is evident that every poet must
have possessed some acquaintance with the art
which was by them inseparably connected with

---

* See GROTE's *History of Greece* and DONALDSON's *Greek
Theatre.*

† *Xenophon. Symp.* ii. 15 and vii.

‡ *De Leg.*, ii. 2–4, vi. 15, vii. 6, and elsewhere.

music and verse. The Greeks reverenced beauty, and an art which made the naturally beautiful appear still more beautiful was not likely to be by them disesteemed. We are told by Athenæus that they brought it to such perfection that "the most eminent sculptors thought their time not ill employed in studying and drawing the attitudes of their public dancers," a study to which he attributes much of the transcendent beauty of their productions.

From the Pæan, or choral dance of Apollo, developed the Gymnopædic, the Pyrrhic, and the Hyporchematic dances. To the first of these I have already more than once alluded. It was regarded as a kind of introduction to the second. At the festival of the gymnopædia there were large choruses of men and boys, a great number of the inhabitants of the city taking part in the dancing. "It was," says Müller, "at these great city choruses that those of blemished reputation always occupied the hindermost rows. Sometimes, nevertheless, men of consideration, when placed there by the arranger of the chorus, boasted that they did honour to the places; the places did not dishonour them."* Thus

* *History of the Doric Race.*

we may see in what high reputation these exhibitions
were held by the Lacedæmonians, notwithstanding
the fact that the performers were entirely unclad.
The men and boys danced in separate choirs. The
choragus, or leader, was crowned with palm leaves,
and it was the privilege of this individual to defray
the expenses of the chorus.

All who took part in the gymnopædia were
thoroughly well-trained dancers, as it was one of
the customs enjoined by Lycurgus that all Spartan
children should commence to receive instruction in
the art from the age of five.

The Spartans are not credited by Aristotle with
a profound scientific knowledge of music, but only
with taste and a just discrimination for the art.
Müller, however, is of opinion that music must have
been generally cultivated by the Dorians and the
kindred race of Arcadians from the circumstance
that "women took part in it, and sang and danced
in public, both with men and by themselves."
Music and dancing—the latter including gymnastics
and wrestling—were indeed the only accomplishments taught to the females of the Laconian capital,
since spinning, sewing, and the milder duties of
domestic life to which Athenian women devoted

themselves were regarded by the Spartans as slavish
and degrading occupations.

It appears that at some of the festivals instituted
by Lycurgus three great choruses were formed: of
boys, of young men, and of old men. The old
men began the dance, singing how they had, in
days gone by, been strong and valiant; then the
young men took up the theme, answering that they
could now accomplish feats as great as any that had
yet been done; and lastly the children sang how,
when their time came, they hoped to surpass both
in deeds of valour and glory.

Athenæus says that the *Gymnopædica* resembled
the dance which "by the ancients used to be called
Anapale," or "Wrestling Dance"; and, according to
Aristoxenus, after exercising themselves in the
Gymnopædica, the performers turned to the *Pyrrhic*
Dance before they entered the theatre.

The last mentioned, which is, perhaps, the most
famous of all the Greek dances, is supposed by
some to have been originally founded on the
Memphitic Dance of Egypt, the same which
Socrates is said to have been fond of practising.
Lucian attributes the invention of the *Pyrrhic*
Dance to Neoptolemus, the son of Achilles, who,

he says, "so much excelled in the art of dancing
that he enriched it with a fine new species, which,
from his surname,* received the appellation Pyr-
rhichia."† It is a very difficult matter to arrive
at the true origin of any dance, either ancient or
modern; but from whatever source the Pyrrhic
or war dance of the Greeks, and subsequently of
the Romans, may have developed, it is certain
that its influence must have extended to the remotest and most barbarous nations, and that in
some form it has continued among the Greeks
themselves even to modern times.

"You have the Pyrrhic Dance as yet," sings
Byron in his "Isles of Greece."‡ But even so
far back as the time of Athenæus (second century
A.D.) the nature of the dance must have undergone
considerable modification, for he says, "But the
Pyrrhic as it exists in our own time appears to
be a sort of Bacchic dance, and a little more pacific
than the old one; for the dancers carry thyrsi
instead of spears, and they point and dart canes

* Pyrrhicus or Pyrrhus.—*Vide* Pausanias, book x., chap. 26.
† *Dialogue de Saltat.* See also Athenæus (xiv. 28), quoting
Aristoxenus. Pliny (vii. 57) attributes the invention to Pyrrhus.
‡ *Don Juan,* canto iii.

at one another, and carry torches. And they dance
figures having reference to Bacchus and the
Indians, and to the story of Pentheus; and they
require for the Pyrrhic Dance the most beautiful
airs."*

Of the extraordinary influence which the practice
of dancing has had *even upon the history of nations*,
we may infer something from a remarkable statement made by the ancient writer above quoted,
who, after informing us that the Pyrrhic Dance
"has not been preserved among any other people
of Greece except the Lacedæmonians," goes on to
say, "*And since that has fallen into disuse their wars
have been brought to a conclusion*," thus connecting
the warlike propensities of the people with their
cultivation of this particular dance.

In the Pyrrhic Dance, as it was performed at
Sparta in the time of her greatness, real arms
were always employed; the figures of the dance
represented a kind of mimic battle, and the movements of the dancers were generally light, rapid,
and eminently characteristic. There were, for
instance, figures representing pursuit of an enemy
or retreat, accompanied naturally by rapid actions

* *Deipnosophists*, xiv. 29.

of the limbs; there were movements and positions
of the body by which spear thrusts, darts, and
wounds generally could be best avoided; and aggres-
sive actions, such as striking with the sword, hurl-
ing the javelin, etc., were cleverly imitated, with
appropriate attitudes. And all these movements
were performed in the most accurate time to the
music of flutes.

It is easy to perceive how the constant practice
of such dances by youths from their earliest years
was calculated to impart to them precision of movement, suppleness of body, pliant yet firm action
of the limbs, celerity of motion, and all those
physical qualities that would be most advantageous
in close-handed warfare,* besides enabling them
to perform the evolutions of battle simultaneously
and in regular order.

* " Now the quickness of the body is, of all things, the most
appertaining to war, one kind connected with the feet, the other
with the hands."—PLATO, *Laws*, bk. viii. chap. 4.

That perfect command over the muscles which renders it
possible for a person to keep one limb perfectly firm while the
opposite member is perfectly pliant, and at a given signal to
change the relative action of the limbs so that the one that
was previously rigid becomes relaxed, and the one that was
pliant becomes firm, forms, so to speak, the acme of muscle
culture, and can only be obtained by constant and well-regulated
practice.

The appearance of young women in these dances may sometimes have formed a kind of interlude, and sometimes they may have mingled with the youths; but that they did occasionally join in them is certain. *Mulieres etiam saltant, una alteram manu tenentes,* says Strabo in the third book of his geography, and the fact is mentioned by Athenæus, Plutarch, and many ancient writers. The customs of the Spartans and Dorians generally permitted the freest intercourse between young people of both sexes, who were specially brought in contact at the great religious festivals and choruses. It seems that in these early times, as in the later days of chivalry, the youths who had distinguished themselves at these mimic contests or dances desired no greater reward than smiles of approbation from the maidens present, and dreaded nothing so much as their derision or contempt. Unfortunately, nowadays young men do not appear to have the same wholesome dread of making themselves ridiculous in the presence of the fair sex. They will not even learn to dance decently, much less trouble to attain anything like excellence.

The third dance mentioned in connection with the worship of Apollo was the Hyporchema

($\dot{v}\pi o\rho\chi\eta\mu a$), which, besides the chorus, consisted
of persons who added an appropriate pantomimic
display.* But there appear to have been dances
of different kinds included under this general term.
Athenæus says, "The Hyporchematic Dance is that
in which the chorus dances while singing."† In
another place he tells us that, like the *cordax*, it
is a dance of a sportive character, and, in illustration of the bodily activity required for its performance, he quotes Bacchylides, saying, "There's
no room now for sitting down ; there's no room
for delay." He also says, "It is a dance for men
and women, and a favourite among the maidens
of Lacedæmon," allusion to which fact may also
be found in the odes of Pindar. A mimetic dance
of this nature is described by Xenophon in the
sixth book of his *Anabases*, and also by Athenæus
thus : "After libations were made, and the guests
had sung a pæan, there rose up first the Thracians,
and danced in arms to the music of a flute, and
jumped up very high with light jumps, and used
their swords. And at last one of them strikes
another, so that it seemed to everyone that the

* Fosbroke's *Antiquities*.
† Book xiv.

F

man was wounded; and he fell down in a very
clever manner, and all the bystanders raised an
outcry. And he who struck him, having stripped
him of his arms, went out singing *sitacles;* and
others of the Thracians carried out his antagonist
as if he were dead, but in reality he was not hurt.
After this some Ænianians and Magnesians rose
up, who danced the dance called Carpæa, they too
being in armour. And the fashion of the dance
was like this: One man, having laid aside his arms,
is sowing and driving a yoke of oxen, constantly
looking round, as if he were afraid. Then comes
up a robber; but the sower, as soon as he sees
him, snatches up his arms, and fights in defence
of his team in regular time to the music of the
flute, and at last the robber, having bound the
man, carries off the team; but sometimes the sower
conquers the robber, and then, binding him along-
side his oxen, he ties his hands behind him and
drives him forward."

Another mimetic dance is described by Xenophon
as being performed towards the close of an entertainment given by Callias to divert his guests,
among whom was Socrates. It represented the
marriage of Dionysus and Ariadne. A very in-

teresting and quaint account of this performance
is given by Robert Burton in the chapter on love
melancholy in his famous *Anatomy.* " First," says
he, " Ariadne, dressed like a bride, came in and
took her place. By-and-by Dionysus entered,
dancing to the music. The spectators did all
admire the young man's carriage, and Ariadne
herself was so affected with the sight that she
could scarcely sit. After a while Dionysus, be-
holding Ariadne, and, incensed with love, bowing
to her knees, embraced her first, and kissed her
with a grace. She embraced him again, and kissed
him with the like affection," etc. The inquiring
male reader who would learn the conclusion of
this dance, and the effect produced thereby upon
the spectators, must refer to the pages of *Democritus
Junior.* I have quoted quite sufficient to show
that the performance must have been of a particularly tender and characteristic nature. It was
a specimen of that wonderful pantomimic art in
which the Greeks so greatly excelled, and which
has already been alluded to in the opening chapter.

It would be impossible in these pages to give a
detailed account of all the dances of which mention
is made by the ancient writers. The ones already

treated of appear to have attained the greatest
celebrity. Athenæus speaks of a dance in use
among private individuals called *anthema* (ἄνθεμα),
in dancing which, he says, they repeated the following words with a kind of mimicking gesture :—

> "Oh where are my roses, oh where are my violets?
>   And where is my beautiful parsley?
>   Are these, then, my roses? are these, then, my violets?
>   And is this my beautiful parsley?"

But this was probably a sort of game among them
similar to those introduced at juvenile parties, such
as "Oranges and lemons" or "Here we go round
the mulberry bush." The same writer also enumerates some dances which, he says, were of a ridiculous
character, and among others he mentions the *Mor-
phasmus*, the *Owl and the Lion*, the *Pouring out of
Meal*, the *Abolition of Debt*, and the *Taking hold of
Wood*, all of which appear to be figure dances of a
similar nature to those already alluded to as being
in use among the Egyptians. The *Scope Scopuma*
was a figure in which the dancers put their hand
to their eyes, making an arch over the brows, as
if looking out into the distance. The *Monocheros*
was the Greek hornpipe. In the *Thermastris* the
dancer executed high jumps, in which, ere the

feet came to the ground, several capers were to be cut.* The Deimalea was danced in a circle. The Ithymbi was danced to Dionysus, and the Dance of the Caryatides was dedicated to Diana. The Hypogypones was a Laconian dance, in which the movements of old men with sticks were imitated; the Gypones was performed on wooden stilts, the dancers wearing transparent Tarentine dresses; and there was a Deicelistic dance, in which were mimicked the actions of those caught stealing the remains of meals.†

This last-mentioned dance is one which we should naturally incline to consider as being of a specially puerile and undignified nature, if we did not bear in mind the fact that among the Spartans it was not considered by any means disgraceful for youths to steal provisions so long as the theft was accomplished without discovery. Indeed, they were sometimes kept short of food, so that they might be driven by hunger to steal from the messes of the men, or even to plunder private houses. This was done with the idea of making them sharp; but while, if successful in their predatory excursions,

* Eustath. ad Odyss., viii. 264.
† Lucian, Athenæus, Müller, Fosbroke, Smith, etc.

they were permitted to retain the spoil, and were even honoured with praise, on the other hand, if caught in the act, they were severely punished, not for the attempt, but for clumsiness in allowing themselves to be detected.

Let us now glance briefly at the dramatic dancing of the ancient Greeks, whose theatres were built large enough to contain the whole population of a city, those of Athens and Sparta being probably the largest.

In Greece the theatre was, we are told, not merely, as with us, a place of entertainment: it was a temple of the god, whose altar was the central part of the vast semicircle of seats from which some thirty thousand of his worshippers sat during a few days in spring, from sunrise to sunset, to gaze upon a spectacle instituted in his honour.* Lucian mentions how even the Bacchanalian Dance was made so serious a concern in Ionia and elsewhere, that so soon as the stated time came round, the people "would sit whole days in the theatre to view the Titans and Corybantes, Satyrs and shepherds"; and he adds, "The most curious part of it is that the most noble and

* See Dr. DONALDSON'S *Theatre of the Greeks.*

greatest personages in every city are the dancers, and so little are they ashamed of it that they applaud themselves more upon their dexterity in that species of talent than on their nobility, their posts of honour, and the dignities of their forefathers." *

The Satyric Dance consisted of rapid and sprightly movements, such as have already been described ; but of the more tragic kind *emmeleia*, the most remarkable, was perhaps the dance of the Eumenedes or Erinnyes. This dance, as it was produced on the Athenian stage, is said to have been so terribly realistic that many of the spectators rushed affrighted from the theatre, imagining that they really beheld the dread sisters whose very names even they did not dare to mention. These awful ministers of divine vengeance, who were supposed to punish the guilty both on earth and in the infernal regions, appeared in black and blood-stained garments. Their aspect was frightful, and their countenances livid with the hue of death. Their heads were wreathed around with serpents in the place of hair, and in their hands they carried a whip of scorpions and a burning torch. Repre-

* *Dialogue de Saltat.*

sented thus, we can scarcely wonder that the dance
of the mimic Furies should have struck terror into
the hearts .of people who believed in the real
existence of such beings.

It has been already stated that the *choragus*, or
leader of the chorus, was one of the most important
personages in connection with the Greek drama,
and that dancers who excelled in pantomimic art
were highly esteemed by the people; but should
a performer be so unfortunate as to fail in his
efforts to please, he was likely to have rather a
bad time of it, since the audience were accustomed
to express disapprobation in a very decided manner.
A bad dancer or actor not only had to put up with
a good deal of chaff, but he ran the risk of being
pelted with stones.

Returning to the more social aspects of Greek
dancing, it is undoubtedly a fact that marriages
were not unfrequently brought about through its
instrumentality. It was ostensibly for this purpose
that young people of both sexes were allowed to
mix together so freely at the great festivals of
Lacedæmon, and even the serious Plato suggests
that "for the sake of this object" (marriage) "it is
necessary for youths and maidens to make them-

selves sports by dancing together." * But there is
one memorable instance on record in which an
exhibition of dancing had precisely the opposite
effect, and caused a young gentleman of some distinction to lose a charming bride who would
certainly otherwise have been his.

The story, which I will endeavour briefly to relate,
is from the sixth book of Herodotus, fancifully
named after the muse Erato.

It appears that Clisthenes, who was the last
tyrant of Sicyon, having himself been victor in the
chariot race at the Olympian games, made a pro-
clamation that he would give his daughter Agarista
in marriage to the man who should prove himself
the most accomplished among the noble youths of
Greece. And for this purpose he invited all who
considered themselves worthy to become his son-in-
law to come to Sicyon, that he might entertain them
at his court and test their merit in all possible
ways.

Herodotus enumerates various suitors who presented themselves; but it will be sufficient for our
purpose to mention two only : Megacles, son of

* Plato, *De Leg.*, vi. 15. His next suggestion appears a little
peculiar.

Alcmæon, and Hippocleides, son of Tisander. These
young men, among many others, remained with
Clisthenes a whole year, during which he had
ample opportunities of observing their disposition
and also of trying their skill in manly accomplishments. It seems that after much deliberation the
choice of the lady's father lay between the two
suitors I have named, and of these Hippocleides was
preferred.*

When at length the day came on which Clisthenes
was to make known his selection, the day, in fact,
on which the marriage was to be actually con-
summated, a more than usually magnificent banquet
and entertainment was prepared, to which all the
Sicyonians were invited. After the feast the suitors
competed in the subjects of eloquence and music.
Up to this time none of the other candidates appear
to have had a chance against Hippocleides, but now
it unfortunately occurred to the young man, who
perhaps had been partaking somewhat freely of
fluid refreshment (and it must be remembered that
the Greeks did not drink from the edge of the
goblet as we do), that it might be well to start a

---

* "He had all the rest in his hands."—*Vide* note to Greek text
Bib. Clar. Ed., G. LONG, M.A.

little entertainment on his own account, to show off his talent for dancing. Accordingly he ordered the musicians to play for him, and began the performance with a stately measure.

Now it happened that Clisthenes himself was by no means ignorant of the choric art, and had his would-be son-in-law confined himself to the serious order of dance,* all might yet have been well; but having displayed his gracefulness, and finding that the company were applauding his efforts, he must needs exhibit something of his agility. So, having rested awhile, he ordered one of the attendants to bring in a table, and mounting thereon, he began to dance Laconian figures, and then proceeded to make all kinds of leaping movements. Clisthenes now began to look askance at the performance, but still restrained himself from openly expressing his disapprobation. Soon, however, the dance degenerated into mere tumbling, and when at last, to crown all, Hippocleides stood upon his head and gesticulated with his legs, Clisthenes could hold out no longer, but exclaimed sharply, "Son of Tisander, you have danced away your marriage." To this the young man very ungraciously replied, "No matter to

* In the text ἐμμέλεια.

Hippocleides!"—a remark which seemed so curious
in the circumstances that it passed into a proverb,*
and was afterwards applied by the Greeks to persons
who were so light-hearted as to allow no misfortune
to affect them even for a moment. There is, of
course, just a possibility that Hippocleides may have
seen something in Agarista not quite to his liking,
and may purposely have made a fool of himself, with
the deliberate intention of disgusting the lady's
father. But even in this case his conduct was
inexcusable, since he could surely have withdrawn
his pretensions to her hand in a more dignified
manner. As it was, the maiden was given to
Megacles, son of Alcmæon, and thus became the
ancestress of the renowned Pericles.

By way of contrast to the folly of Hippocleides,
attention may be drawn to the sensible course
adopted by Hegesianax of Alexandria when he was
present at an entertainment given by Antiochus the
Great, at which the monarch and all his friends
joined in dancing. As soon as it came to the turn
of Hegesianax, and the King asked him to perform
his part, the historian, whose choric skill was not of
the highest order, replied: "Do you wish, O king,

* "Οὐ φροντὶς Ἱπποκλείδῃ!"

to see me dance badly, or would you prefer hearing
me recite my own poems very well?" Antiochus
seems to have preferred the latter alternative, and
so artfully did Hegesianax sing the King's praises
that he not only received a substantial reward, but
was afterwards thought worthy to be ranked among
the King's personal friends.

CHAPTER IV.

DANCING IN ANCIENT ROME.

IN the early days of Rome, when the inhabitants of the city were renowned for the austerity of their morals, dancing appears to have been far more generally practised and more highly esteemed as a pastime for private individuals than it was in those later days of luxury and vice which preceded the downfall of the empire. Under the republic, and especially during the intervals of the Punic wars, dancing in Rome, as in Greece, was considered an essential branch of education, and the children of patricians and senators attended schools to receive instruction in the art. This we learn from Macrobius; and Quintilian, in his *Institutes of Oratory,* also states that "dancing was thought no disgrace to the ancient Romans." He also quotes a remark of Crassus in the third book of Cicero, *De Oratore,* in which he recommends that the actions of the body

should be learnt "not from the theatre and player,
but from the camp and from the *palœstra.*"

Now it was in the *palœstra* that *chironomia,* or
the art of making gestures in a graceful manner,
was taught; and Quintilian, although he lived in
the time of Domitian, when dancing was seldom
practised except by hired performers, pays nevertheless an almost involuntary tribute to the art, and to
the benefit derivable from its cultivation in early
youth, when, in concluding the chapter, he says: " I
do not wish the gesture of an orator to resemble
that of a dancer, but I would have some influence
from such juvenile exercises left, so that the gracefulness communicated to us while we were learning
may secretly attend us when we are not thinking of
our movements."*

One of the most ancient dances practised by the
Romans was called *Bellicrepa saltatio.* It was, as
the name implies, a military dance, and is said to
have been instituted by Romulus after the seizure
of the Sabine women, in order that a similar misfortune might never befall his own state. † The
Pyrrhic Dance was also a Roman institution, and

---

* QUINTILIAN's *Institutes of Oratory,* book i., chap. xii. 19.
† See SMITH's *Antiquities.*

retained its popularity a considerable time, as we
may glean from the fact that Julius Scaliger, when
a youth, often danced it before the Emperor Maxi-
milian, who on one occasion remarked that "the
boy must either have been born in a coat of mail,
or else he had been rocked in one in lieu of a
cradle."

The sacred dances of the Romans developed from
those of the Greeks, which were supposed to have
been introduced from Egypt by Orpheus and
Musæus. To Numa Pompilius, the gentle Sabine,
who became king after the miraculous disappearance
of Romulus, are ascribed the religious institutions
of the Romans, and conspicuous among them was
that of the Salii, or dancing priests of Mars. Of
these he selected twelve from citizens of the first
rank, and gave them the distinction of an em-
broidered tunic and brazen breastplate. In one
hand they held a javelin, while in the other they
carried the celestial shield called *ancilia,* and thus
they went through the city, singing hymns, with
leaping and solemn dancing.*

In most of the sacred festivals of the Romans
dancing formed an important feature, such festivals,

* LIVY, *History,* book i., chap. xx.

for example, as the Agnolia, instituted by Numa in honour of Janus, and the Lupercalia, or festival of Pan, which also commemorated, as some say, the preservation of Romulus and Remus by the wolf. During the Lupercalia it was customary for half-naked youths to rush and dance about the streets with whips, lashing freely all whom they chanced to meet; but the people, especially the women, for superstitious reasons did not mind receiving the lashes, as they imagined particular benefits would follow.

The Rural Dances were also performed in honour of Pan, who was supposed to have been their inventor. The festivals of this god were celebrated during the fine season of the year, and youths and maidens together joined in the dances, which took place in the woods and groves surrounding the city. The heads of the dancers were crowned with wreaths of oak, and across their bodies were thrown garlands of flowers.

At the Palilia, or festival of Pallas, which was solemn and magnificent, dances were held in the fields by shepherds, who during the night formed circles around blazing fires of straw and stubble, singing as they danced, and praying to the goddess

G

for the fruitfulness of their flocks. The feast of
Ceres, or Cerelia, in Rome was similar to the Thes-
mophoria of the Greeks, and the officiators at the
solemnity were free-born women, who appeared
dressed in white robes, emblematical of the most
spotless chastity. *

It is from the Floralia of the Romans that our
old English May Day festival is derived. It was
customary in Rome and other Italian towns for
young men and maidens on the 1st of May to repair
at daybreak to the woods and cut green boughs
from the trees. These they brought back to the
town, and with them decorated the doorways of
their friends' houses. Sometimes they paid a similar
compliment to persons in authority who happened
to be generally esteemed, and in course of time this
became a recognised institution. The persons thus
honoured provided tables for the reception of the
bough - bringers, and the day was passed amid
feasting and gaiety.

In early times the festival of Flora was doubtless
conducted in a sufficiently decent manner, but I
regret to have to state that eventually it degenerated

* OVID, *Met.*, B. x., F. 8. This festival commemorated the
introduction of the laws and regulations of civilised life, which
were generally ascribed to Demeter or Ceres.

into a scene of unbounded licentiousness.* It is said that on one occasion the venerable Cato, who had expressed a desire to witness the celebration, perceived that his presence interrupted the proceedings, as the performers appeared evidently unwilling to shock him. Perceiving this, and not caring to be a spectator of what was to follow, nor yet to put a restraint on the pleasures of others, he decided to retire from the feast. This action on the part of the noble and virtuous senator was appreciated by the young Romans, who, as he left the theatre, greeted him with loud acclamations.

The dances performed in connection with the Dionysia, or orgies of Bacchus, were of a still more reprehensible nature; indeed, the introduction of the worship of this deity contributed greatly to the demoralisation of the Roman people, as it had already of the Greeks, only the Romans carried their indulgence to a far greater extent, beginning, it has been said, where the Greeks left off. All honour, however, is due to the determined action

---

* "The only amusements that at all rivalled the spectacle of the amphitheatre were those which appealed strongly to the sensual passions, such as the games of Flora, the postures of the pantomimes, and the ballet."—LECKY, *History European Morals,* vol. i., p. 276.

of the consuls Albinus and Philippus, who, having made a strict inquiry into the nature of the proceedings consequent upon the revelations of the girl Fecenia Hispala, caused the bacchanalians to be for ever banished from Rome by a decree of the senate. Fecenia had in the first instance been induced to break the oath of secrecy by which initiates were forbidden to divulge what they witnessed at these rites, in order to save her lover from being degraded and ruined by taking part in them; but she was protected from the consequences of her act by the consul, and was afterwards rewarded as a public benefactress. *

An account of ancient dances, which included only such as were praiseworthy, would be of but small value for purposes of reference, and therefore, in order that the present historical sketch may have some show of completeness, I am compelled to make allusion to a few dances which, from personal appreciation of what is noble and dignified in the art, I would prefer to leave unmentioned. It was the scandalous and wanton character of the nuptial and other dances that caused the expulsion of all professional dancers and teachers of dancing from

* Livy, xxxix. 9, 11–13.

Rome.   It is not necessary to describe these dances.
It is sufficient to say that if they were bad enough
to offend such a reprobate as Tiberius, by whose
command the dancers were expelled, they must
have been bad indeed, especially if we may credit
what is related of him by Tacitus and Suetonius.
It seems, however, that this prince in his younger
days adopted the kind of policy recommended by
Hamlet to his mother, and "assumed a virtue
though he had it not." Publicly he reprimanded
Sestius Gallus for the licentiousness of his entertainments, while privately he made an appointment
to sup with him on the express condition that he
should himself be entertained in the usual manner.*

But if Tiberius pretended to be scandalised by
the depravity of the Roman dances, and dis-
couraged the practice of dancing, his successor—
whose character, it must be confessed, was not a
whit better — appears to have been an ardent
admirer and himself no mere amateur of the art.
"So extremely fond was Caligula," says Suetonius,
"of singing and dancing, that he could not refrain
in the theatre from singing with the tragedians and
imitating the gestures of the actors either by way of

* SUET., *Tib.* xlii.

applause or correction." *　And further we are told
that if, when a celebrated actor was dancing in the
theatre, anyone interrupted the performance by
making the slightest noise, the Emperor would
order the delinquent to be "dragged from his seat
while he thrashed him with his own hands."

It has already been hinted that dancing as a
pastime for the people, and especially for those of
the higher classes, was not much appreciated by
the Romans of later times. Hence Cicero, in his
Philippics, reproaches Mark Antony for having
"disgraced the dignity of the consulship" by
dancing in the Lupercalia; and if we may credit
the statement of the orator that Antony "ran
about the streets naked, and armed with a whip,"
we shall, I think, be quite prepared to admit the
justness of his criticism.

But if dancing was rarely practised as an amusement by private persons of quality in the days of
the empire, it was certainly cultivated to the
highest conceivable perfection on the stage by professional artistes. Perhaps the culminating point
was reached during the comparatively good and
glorious reign of Augustus. The tranquillity of this

* Suet., *Cal.* liv.

age afforded every opportunity for the further
development of the art of descriptive dancing,
which the Romans had borrowed from the Greeks,
and which had already been practised with so much
skill by the celebrated actors Roscius and Esopus
as to call for special commendation from the stately
Cicero. I have already used the word "descriptive"
on one or two occasions in speaking of such dancing,
because the term "pantomime" has come to be
associated with a kind of performance which, compared with the noble art of Roscius and the men of
whom I am about to speak, would appear very
degraded. The word, however, in its true sense
as derived from the Greek, implies "imitation of
everything," and a representation of even the most
solemn subjects by dancing would properly be
termed a pantomime. Thus the *saltatio panto-
mimorum* of the Romans were entire dramatic
representations consisting of dancing and gestures
only, and it was in such performances that the two
famous dancers Pylades and Bathyllus are said to
have excelled all who had been before, and indeed
all who came after, them.

These remarkable men flourished in the Augustan
age, and have been celebrated by many of the

Roman and Greek writers. Athenæus states that
they composed their dances from the *emmeleia*
and *cordax*, the latter, I presume, in its least degenerate form. Pylades adopted the tragic style,
confining himself to grave and tender subjects,
while Bathyllus, who was by birth an Alexandrian,
preferred to represent subjects of a lively nature,
and such as demanded special agility in their
execution. Bathyllus is represented as having been
endowed not only with extraordinary talent, but
also with great personal beauty, and is spoken of by
Juvenal as being the idol of the Roman ladies.* At
first the dancers appear to have performed together
in a friendly spirit of rivalry; but by degrees,
becoming jealous of one another, they parted, and
displayed their talents in different theatres. The
people were divided in their opinions as to which
artiste possessed the greater merit, and separated
into two factions. Thus the games were disturbed
by quarrels which arose out of the rivalry which
existed between these men.† Mecænus, the celebrated Roman knight and friend of Augustus, is
said to have been one of the greatest admirers of
Bathyllus, and the Emperor himself encouraged the

* *Sat.*, vi.   † Tacitus, *Annals*, book i. 54.

performances, thinking it citizen-like to mingle in the pleasures of the people.

It has been said that Bathyllus was still admired in the reign of Nero; but if this may be credited, he must have retained his activity to a very advanced age. However, there are instances on record of other dancers who performed on the Roman stage long after they had reached the allotted threescore and ten Pliny speaks of a mimic actress, named Lucceia, who danced when a hundred years old, and also of one Stephanio—"the first to dance on the stage in comedy descriptive of Roman manners"— who had danced in the secular games celebrated by Augustus, and also in those held during the fourth consulship in the reign of Claudius, an interval of sixty-three years having elapsed between them. Still another instance he gives of an actress, Galeria Copiola, who returned to the stage to dance in the interludes at the votive games celebrated for the health of the deified Augustus, just ninety-one years after her first appearance.* Weaver, in his historical essay, says that in the sports instituted by Nero "an ancient, noble, and rich lady, one Alliamatula, danced at one hundred and twenty

* PLINY, *Natural History*, book vii., chap. 1.

years old"; but he does not, so far as I can remember, give his authority for this remarkable
statement. Athenæus mentions a Macedonian com-
mander of great repute, named Polysperchon, " who,
though a very old man, danced whenever he was
drunk," and who, when once he started, did not
seem readily inclined to stop.* But ability to
exercise saltatory powers does not appear to have
belonged exclusively to the ancients. There is
evidence that our own virgin queen danced gaill-
lardes when she was close on seventy, and the
gaillarde, as its name implies, was a dance of a
particularly lively order. †

Doubtless much of the prejudice that existed
among the Romans against dancing as an accomplishment for private persons, arose from their
practical and utilitarian views. Sallust does not
reproach Sempronia because she was able to
dance, but because she was able to dance with
a degree of perfection that was not considered
necessary for a woman in her station, thereby implying that the time spent in acquiring such per-

* *Deipnosophists*, book iv. 42.

† Tabouret speaks of the gaillarde as being a dance more suitable for young people. The step consisted of an *assemblé*, in
leaping a *pas marché* and *pas tombé*.

fection could have been more profitably employed. In the same sense Plutarch quotes with approval the remark made by Philip of Macedon to his son when he heard him playing with great brilliancy on the harp: "Are you not ashamed to play so well?" *

But, even regarded from a purely utilitarian standpoint, the art of pantomimic dancing was not without its advantages, as the following anecdote will serve to show. A prince of one of the tribes of Pontus, who happened to be staying at the court of Nero, frequently observed one of the dancers, who performed his parts with such perfection that the foreigner, although he could not comprehend a word of what was sung by the chorus, was nevertheless able, by following the actions of the dancer, to understand without difficulty all that he intended to convey. When the time came for the prince's departure, Nero, who is reported to have been of a generous disposition—and perhaps this is the only thing that can be said in his favour—told him that any request he had to make should be granted. To this the prince replied that if Nero would only make him a present of the dancer whom he so

* PLUTARCH, *Life of Pericles.*

greatly admired he would indeed be happy. "And
what would you do with him?" asked the Emperor.
"I have around me," said the prince, "several
neighbouring tribes who speak different languages,
and as they are unable to understand mine, I
thought, if I had this man with me, it would be
quite possible for him to explain by gesture all that
I wished to express."*

The art of pantomimic dancing continued to
flourish in Rome till the sixth century. We are
told that there were as many as three thousand
foreign female dancers employed upon the Roman
stage, and so essential was their presence considered
that at one time when, through scarcity of food, all
strangers—even including orators, philosophers, and
public teachers—were banished from the city, these
dancers were allowed to remain because they contributed so greatly to the pleasures of the people.†

* LUCIAN, *Dialogue de Saltat.*
† AMMIANUS, I. xiv. 6; also GIBBON'S *Decline and Fall,*
chap. xxxi.

CHAPTER V.

RELIGIOUS, MYSTERIOUS, AND FANATICAL ELEMENTS IN DANCING.

THERE are various Scriptural passages which
tend to show that among the Jews dancing
was always regarded as a becoming expression of
religious fervour and joyful emotion. After a great
victory over their enemies it was customary for the
Israelitish women to welcome back their defenders
with dances and songs of triumph. Of this we
may find an example in the history of David, when,
on his return from "the slaughter of the Philistine,"
the women came out from all the cities singing and
dancing, "with tabrets, with joy, and with instruments of music," and aroused Saul's jealousy by
comparing the thousands he had slain with the tens
of thousands slain by David.* Another instance
may be found in the tragic story of Jephthah's

* 1 Samuel xviii.

daughter, who came dancing with gladness to meet her father after his subjection of the children of Ammon, little thinking, poor girl, that she was dancing to her death in consequence of the rash vow which Jephthah had made.*

The dancing of Miriam and her maidens after the passage of the Red Sea has been already referred to in connection with Egyptian dances; but the reader's attention may be called to an apocryphal passage from which we learn that after the victory of Judith over Holofernes the women of Israel assembled to meet her, "and made a dance among them for her," the words implying that it was arranged impromptu for the occasion. Then, we are told, they put a garland of olive upon Judith and her maid, and she herself "went before all the people in the dance, leading all the women," while the men followed in their armour, with garlands and songs.†

Perhaps, however, the most familiar instance of dancing mentioned in the Old Testament is that of David, whose peculiar manner of expressing his gladness before the ark provoked the sarcastic comment of Michal: "How glorious was the king

* Judges xi.   † Judith xv.

of Israel to-day, who uncovered himself to-day in
the eyes of the handmaids of his servants, as one
of the vain fellows shamelessly uncovereth himself."
To this David retorted that it was "before the
Lord" he danced, who had appointed him ruler over
Israel before Michal's father and all his house. The
purport of David's further remarks is not quite so
apparent, but the context would show that Michal
acted wrongly in reproving him.

It has been suggested—I think by Dr. William
Smith—that Saul's daughter felt piqued when she
beheld David enacting the part of *choragus*, because
she was well aware that, according to Jewish custom,
it would have been more fitting if she had herself
led the dance on such an occasion.

Some writers infer from the asperity of Michal's
rebuke that the King of Israel actually danced in
the same condition as Moses when, according to
the Eastern legend, the stone on which he had
placed his clothes ran away with them into the
camp;* or as Sophocles and Mark Antony are
reported to have danced on memorable occasions.
But this inference is not just. David only re-

* This happened in order to remove a scandal which was
rumoured against him. See SALE's Notes to *Al Korân*.

moved such garments as were likely to impede
the vigour of his actions, for it is stated in a previous verse that he danced "with all his might," and
was "girded with a linen ephod."*

It is probable that the dance, as practised by
the Israelites of these early days, was of an extremely simple and unpremeditated character,
bearing some resemblance to that of the Greeks
in the Heroic Age. The leader was generally a
woman or young maiden, of near relationship to
the hero, or of some importance in connection
with the event, who improvised certain figures
and steps, while the rest of the dancers imitated
her example as nearly as possible. Such was the
dancing of Miriam, of Judith, and of the maidens
of Shiloh, who came out unsuspectingly "to dance
in the dances," and were forcibly carried away by
the children of Benjamin, as in after years the
Sabine women were carried away by the young
Romans. All the dances to which attention has
yet been drawn had their origin in religious en-
thusiasm or feelings of joy, and though doubtless
the movements of the dancers were imbued with
a certain natural gracefulness, like those of the

* 2 Sam. vi.

Greek maidens who practised the Dipodia, still they were for the most part unpremeditated and unstudied.

But the dance of Salomê, the daughter of Herodias, is likely to have been a far more elaborate performance, for at that time the pantomimic art had reached its highest perfection, and the influence of the great Roman dancers had already extended far and wide. Besides, her dance had no connection whatever with religious zeal, like those of David or Miriam. It was simply executed in honour of the tetrarch's birthday, and the steps and figures, which were arranged with the special object of displaying the girl's gracefulness and talent, had probably been long and carefully studied beforehand.

The Jews in early times, like the Greeks and Egyptians, introduced dancing into all their great religious festivals. For instance, at the festival of the first-fruits the whole population of a town would turn out. A procession was formed, headed by flute-players, and the virgins danced to the music as they went along. At the feast of Tabernacles or of Ingathering, also, the young people danced around the altar, which was

H

decorated with branches of poplar-osiers. On the
Day of Atonement there was dancing in the
vineyards, and chain dances were formed. Moreover, there were occasions when torchlight dances
were held, and when the most honoured men
danced and hurled their torches into the air and
again caught them as they fell. * When the
children of Israel danced around the golden calf
in the wilderness, we are not told that it was the
fact of their dancing that provoked the anger of
Moses, but simply their idolatry. I am unable
to call to mind any instance throughout the Old
or New Testament where dancing is actually
condemned. On the contrary, it is generally
spoken of approvingly. We are reminded in the
book of Ecclesiastes that "there is a time to
dance." In the book of Jeremiah, when the
return of the Jews from captivity is foretold,
we find the words, "Then shall the virgin re-
joice in the dance, both young men and old
together: for I will turn their mourning into
joy."† The Psalmist exclaims: "Let us praise His
name in the dance," and Jesus Himself uses the

* Dr. FRANK DELITZSCH in the *Expositor.*
† Jer. xxxi. 13.

expression, "We have piped unto you, and ye have not danced." *

It would be altogether beyond the scope of the present chapter to enter into a defence of dancing on religious grounds, but parenthetically I really fail to see how, in face of the above-quoted texts, any orthodox person can consistently aver that dancing itself is a wicked pursuit. Such a person may, perhaps not unreasonably, object to this or that particular form of dance; he may rightly consider that the world would suffer no great loss if the *cancan* were relegated to the limbo of forgotten things; he may even be of opinion that a salutary change would be effected by the elimination of a few of the waltzes from our modern ball programmes; but, whatever may be his prejudices, he has no right to say that all dancing is sinful.

But, to return to our historical considerations, as the Israelites probably derived the custom of dancing at religious ceremonies from their ancient oppressors, the Egyptians, so the early Christians appear to have borrowed their masques and dances from their pagan persecutors. In some of the

* Luke vii. 32.

oldest Roman churches the choir is a kind of
raised stage, and on this the priests are said to
have danced the sacred dances. * It has been
suggested that the first bishops were inclined to
favour religious dancing because they were aware
that the early proselytes to Christianity would not
readily give up a practice which they had been
used to regard as an essential part of worship.

However this may be, as I have elsewhere
stated, the early Christians were not allowed to
give expression to their religious zeal in saltatory
exercise for very long. In consequence of the
scandals connected with their Agapæ, or love-
feasts, which frequently took place at night, and
to which allusion is made by St. Jude when he
says, "These are spots on your feasts of charity,"
dancing fell into discredit. It was denounced by
St. Augustine and St. Chrysostom, as it had
already been denounced by Tertullian and other
writers, and was at length prohibited by the Church.
The practice, however, appears to have revived, and
so late as the seventh century a prohibitive decree
of the council was published containing special

---

* Scaliger says that the early bishops were called *præsules*,
because they originally led the dance in solemn festivals.

clauses against "the public or objectionable dances of women, and festivities in honour of false gods." The priesthood encouraged the notion that the devil was the special patron of the dance, indeed its originator, as St. Chrysostom averred; and dancing was declared to have been accursed ever since the day when Salomê, by her graceful performance, induced the Tetrarch to gratify her mother's cruel desire.*

The communities of the Waldenses and Albigenses, which appeared in the twelfth century, were most determinedly opposed to any form of dancing. Their sentiments with regard to this form of amusement were very forcibly expressed in their ordinances, in which may be found clauses not only condemning the practice of dancing, but which appear, to say the least, somewhat rough on the ladies. For example, we are not only informed that a dance is "the devil's procession," that "of dancing the devil is the guide, the middle, and the end," but we learn that "in the dance the

* John Chrysostom, the saint of the "golden mouth," according to Gibbon, incurred the enmity of the Empress Eudoxia by the exordium of a sermon : "Herodias is again furious. Herodias again dances ; she once more requires the head of John."—*Decline and Fall*, chap. xxxii.

devil useth the strongest armour that he has, for
his most powerful arms are women, which is made
plain to us in that he made choice of the woman
to deceive the first man." After this conclusive
evidence one would think enough had been said,
but we are further assured that "women come
not readily to the dance if they be not painted
and admired." (Remember, please, that this statement was made some hundreds of years since, and
has no reference whatever to modern society.) So
far as male dancers are concerned, the ordinance
affirms that "he who entereth a good and wise
man into a dance cometh forth a corrupt and
wicked man."*

The extravagant notion of the Albigenses, that
dancing was a special arrangement of the devil's
to beguile humanity from more serious pursuits,
will not, perhaps, appear so strange if we consider
the nature of their tenets. They belonged to
that division of the Cathari who believed that
primal matter was created by the supreme Father, the
one eternal principle; but that after his rebellion

---

* Petrarch says : " *Incitamentum libidinus chorœa—circulus e
ejus centrum diabolus.*" But why the Italian poet should have
been so bitter against dancing I fail to discover.

and fall, the Evil Being was empowered to arrange this original matter according to his own fancy. Consequently, according to their ideas, all things appertaining to the material world, even our own human bodies, were the design and production of the principle of evil. Believing this, it followed, as a natural consequence, that whatever proved gratifying to the senses in any form was held by them to be more or less accursed.

About the year 1373 there originated at Aix-la-Chapelle a sect which Mosheim, in his *Ecclesiastical History*, describes as the Dancers. "Persons of both sexes," says this writer, "publicly and in private houses, suddenly broke out into a dance, and, holding each other by the hand, danced with great violence till they fell down nearly exhausted." Further, we learn that those who were thus attacked declared themselves to be favoured with wonderful visions.* This dancing madness, we are told, spread through the districts of Liege, Hainault, and the Belgian provinces. Another writer relates that hundreds of people danced involuntary maniac dances down the streets, while

* MOSHEIM, *Ecclesiastical History*, Part II, chap. v. See also ROBERTSON'S *History of the Church*, p. 119.

others within doors seemed smitten with the
epidemic, and rushed from their houses to join
the dancing crew, unable to resist the frantic
impulse. It seems that victims of this dancing
mania not unfrequently died from exhaustion consequent upon their unwonted and frenzied efforts.

Almost immediately following this outbreak—
which, strange to say, originated in the same
year as the terrible scourge known as the Black
Pest—came a grotesque and gruesome performance
known as the Dance Macabre, or, perhaps, more
familiarly as the "Dance of Death." The word
Macabre is supposed to have been a corruption of
Macarius, the name of the saint to whom the
dance was dedicated. In England it was also
called the "shaking of the sheet," a name which
doubtless originated from some characteristic pantomime which formed part of the performance.

Perhaps in its original form this singularly re-
pulsive dance—which appears to have obtained a
considerable vogue during the fourteenth century,
and to have spread in some form throughout
Europe—was intended to convey a highly moral
lesson; but it is certain that eventually it degenerated into a scene of the wildest and most
ribald description.

The Dance Macabre, as it is said to have been
performed in the Cemetière des Innocents by
people whose homes had actually been rendered
desolate by war, famine, and pestilence, must
have presented a truly hideous spectacle. Mum-
mers were dressed, we are told, to typify the
various orders of humanity, from the monarch to
the beggar, and each representative was led by
a companion mummer, dressed in black and painted
to resemble a skeleton, the head being covered
with a skull-like mask. In this manner the dancers
went up the centre walk of the cemetery, each
skeleton endeavouring to rival its fellow in the
execution of grotesque and distorted antics; and
so callous had the hearts of the people become,
from long familiarity with the reality of death in
its most hideous form, that this disgusting mockery
was actually described as being "mightily laughable
and diverting."*

* There are, I regret to say, even in this enlightened century,
people who imagine that there is something "mightily laughable
and diverting" in mimic representations of the sad emblems of
mortality, especially if they be illuminated with coloured fire. To
a certain order of intelligence, a painted skull, with lights blazing
through the eyeless sockets, would seem to be a particularly droll
object. Not long since I was present at an entertainment where
the proceedings terminated with the entrance of a gigantic skeleton robed in a winding-sheet. And this entertainment was given

Notwithstanding the efforts made by the bishops, and notably by Odo of Paris, in the twelfth century to suppress sacred and ecclesiastical dances, they appear to have been practised in a modified form in some foreign countries to within comparatively recent times. In France they were finally abolished by a parliamentary decree bearing date September 3rd, 1687, and we read that until about this time it was customary at the grand fête of St. Martial for the people of Limoges to dance

ostensibly *for the amusement of children !* What a spectacle to present to their gaze, the last, too, on which their eyes rested before leaving the theatre ! what execrable taste ! Let us concede that fairies, gnomes, demons even, dwelling as they do only in the realms of fancy, are perfectly legitimate objects to stimulate the imagination and excite the wonder of children ; but the secrets of the grave should be respected, and whatever has reference to the awful reality of death— phantoms, skeletons, and such things —ought not to be paraded before their young eyes. Managers of theatres should reflect that among their audience there may be some little ones to whom such representations are likely to prove no laughing matter ; that although the brave little creatures may appear not to be frightened while others are near, yet, all the same, the objects they have seen may haunt their dreams by night and inspire their wakeful hours with terror. It is cruel to frighten children, or allow them to be frightened. Let parents read Elia's beautiful essay on witches, wherein he speaks of the strange terrors that surround the years of sinless childhood, and, mindful of the health and happiness of their little ones, carefully avoid taking them to any entertainments where ghastly objects are exhibited.

a round in the church of St. Leonard, singing in
their own dialect : "*San Marcàu, prija per noû, et
noû epingoran per voû*," in place of the *Gloria
Patri et Filio.* About the beginning of the sixteenth century Francis Cisneros, or, as he is
perhaps more familiarly called, Cardinal Ximenez,
is said to have restored the old custom at Toledo
of performing dances in the cathedral choir during
Mass—a custom which had been originally instituted by Saint Isidor of Seville in the seventh
century.

An anonymous contributor to the *St. James'
Magazine*, writing about fifty years since, states
that "in the cathedral of Seville a ballet is performed nightly during the *ottave del corpus* in front
of the high altar." The dancers, he says, are
"boys varying in age from twelve to sixteen,
dressed in the rich old Spanish garb, and the
movements are stately and measured." It is said
that this practice continues to the present day at
Seville, and I read that a dance is also held in the
abbey church of Echternach on the occasion of the
Feast of St. Willibrod.

Religious dancing of the fanatical order is still
practised by certain sects. The dervishes of the

East continue to gyrate as wildly as ever they did; but other enthusiasts have wisely modified the nature of their choric performances. The Shakers, who originated in Lancashire about the year 1747, but are now more widely distributed in the United States, have long since discontinued the violent shakings and bodily contortions by which they acquired their name, and have substituted a rhythmic and not undignified dance around the place of worship, accompanying their movements, as did the Egyptians and Israelites of old, by singing and the clapping of hands.

Some of the minor communities which spring up from time to time—as, for instance, the "Army of the Lord," whose peculiarities not a great while ago scandalised the town of Brighton—appear to make a great feature of saltatory exercise. Indeed, like those unfortunate people who were attacked by the St. Vitus's dance in the fourteenth century, they will sometimes continue moving till they positively fall fainting from exhaustion.

CHAPTER VI.

REMARKABLE DANCES OF LATER TIMES.

IN considering the dances of the ancient world,
I dwelt at greater length on those of Greece,
because that country is regarded as the cradle of
the arts; and the influence of the Greeks on
dancing, as well as on painting and literature, will
endure for all time, or at least so long as ever there
are teachers of cultivated taste.

We still delight to study and imitate the attitudes
of Greek dancers, as transmitted to us in marble
by Praxiteles and other ancient sculptors whose
matchless works outlive their names; and doubtless
we should delight to practise their dances also, if
any reliable choregraphy of them were available.
But, alas! such is not the case, and though it may
not be difficult for a student well versed in the
traditions of his art to form a fairly accurate
conception of the steps and figures which the

Greeks employed, no honest writer would care to
vouch for their actual progression and sequence.

With regard, however, to the dances which are
now about to claim our attention, one is able to
speak more definitely. Indeed, I may say that
by diligent research in every available source of
information, and by conscientious study of some
old and rare works bearing directly upon the subject, it would be possible for anyone acquainted
with those traditional theories and rules which
have been handed down to us from generation to
generation—and which, as I have already shown,
have varied but little during three thousand years
—to reproduce many of them almost exactly in
their original form.

But clearly it would not be possible in the
present work to describe in detail all, or indeed
even a small part, of the dances which have
obtained popularity since the period of the
Renaissance, when dancing with other arts began
to revive. A mere catalogue of dances which have
found favour in England alone would fill many
pages, to say nothing of those of other countries.
It is, therefore, my intention to select only the
most remarkable among them, entering more

minutely into the details of some and dismissing others with a few words.

The occasion which gave the necessary impetus to the revival of dancing as a cultivated art in Europe was, we are told, a magnificent fête or ballet given at Tortona by an Italian nobleman to celebrate the marriage between Isabella of Aragon and Galeazzo, Duke of Milan. It would seem that every resource that wealth and genius could supply was brought into requisition at this entertainment, and that all the arts were advanced thereby. The spirit of emulation was awakened, and princes and nobles of surrounding cities and countries vied with each other in the magnificence of their entertainments, and imitating the example of Bergonzo de Botta, encouraged exhibitions of choric and historic skill.

Catherine de Medicis, although one of the worst sovereigns who have figured in history, possessed at least one redeeming quality: her love and patronage of literature and the fine arts. It was to this queen that dancing was greatly indebted for its advancement in France. She gave the ladies of her court opportunities of displaying their gracefulness by adding to the solemn old *basses danses,*

including the *branle* and *pavane*, movements of a
livelier nature, such as the *tourdion gaillarde* and
volta, to all of which I shall call more particular
attention as we proceed.

It may be that the encouragement given by
Catherine to the particular art we are now considering was not entirely disinterested; indeed,
it has been suggested that she introduced dances
which were not always conspicuous for their propriety in order to exert an enervating influence
on her son's mind, and divert his attention from
the affairs of government. Tournaments, which
had become unfashionable since Henry II. had
lost a limb through taking part in one, were now
superseded by grand ballets and allegories, and in
the year 1581 a costly entertainment of this
description was produced under the auspices of
the court, when the Duc de Joyeuse, favourite of
Henry III., was united to the Queen's sister. In
honour of this event, the Queen herself also gave
at the Louvre a splendid fête, at which was performed a ballet representing Ceres and her nymphs.

During the reign of Henry IV. it was customary
for princes, nobles, and their ladies to practise
ballets the whole year through, in order to perfect

themselves in their parts, and rival each other in the splendour of their productions.* The Queen, Marie de Medicis, was a great lover of dancing. She frequently performed in the court ballets, and was conspicuous by the dignity of her bearing and the richness of her attire. On one occasion her Majesty herself composed a ballet in honour of Madame de Verneuil,† which was executed by fifteen of the most beautiful of the court ladies. In the course of this ballet, after the second *entrée*, the Queen and the favourite appeared together in the midst of the dancers, thus proclaiming the kindly feeling which, strange to say, at that time existed between them.

The nuncio of the Pope assisted at this spectacle, and the King, who was near to him, remarking the magnificence of the costumes worn by the per-

* *Memoires de Mareschal de Bassompierre.* The author himself first attracted the King's notice while taking part in a ballet. An introduction was effected, with the result that a warm friendship sprang up on both sides. Bassompierre was an exquisite dancer, and not only was he generally highly accomplished, but was also greatly distinguished for personal beauty. Like Bathyllius of Alexandria, he appears to have been a general favourite with the ladies, for he tells us that the day before his arrest he burnt upwards of *six thousand love-letters* which he had received at different times from his female admirers.

† Henrietta de Balzac d'Entragues.

I

formers and the glitter of their jewels, turned and
asked "*S'il avait jamais vu un pareil escadron.*"
"*Sire,*" replied the ambassador, "*je n'en ai jamais
vu de plus beau, ni de plus dangereux.*" *

The great monarch himself was as ardent an
admirer of the ballet as either of his consorts,
and many superb and costly fêtes were given
during the twenty years of his reign. The taste
for this form of entertainment continued un-
abated, and Henry's successors, Louis XIII. and
Louis XIV., both performed publicly in ballets.
The latter is indeed reported to have been a most
excellent dancer, and this is not perhaps to be
wondered at, seeing that for more than twenty
years he regularly received lessons of the celebrated
Beauchamp.† Until he reached his thirty-second
year the King is said to have taken part in nearly
all the court ballets, but feeling piqued by some
verses referring to Nero's theatrical amusements
which Racine had introduced in his *Britannicus,*
he resolved to give up the practice, and appeared
for the last time on February 13th, 1669, in the
ballet of *Flora.*

* AUGUSTE DE LACROIX. *Les Reines de la Nuit.*
† RAMEAU, *Maître à Danser.*

The patronage of Louis XIV. was extended to all the arts. Music, painting, architecture, and dancing received the highest encouragement; indeed, of the last-mentioned the reign of this monarch has rightly been termed the golden age. A royal academy of dancing was founded in 1661, composed of thirteen of its most celebrated exponents, among whom were "M. Galand du Desert, *maître à danser de la Reine;* M. Prevost, *maître à danser du Roi;* Jean Renaud, *maître à danser de Monsieur frère du Roi; et* Guillaume Raynaud, *maître à danser de Monseigneur le Dauphin.*" With this academy were also associated the names of Molière, Lully, and Philippe Quinault, and the object of its formation was to elevate the art of dancing, to uphold its traditions, to confirm its theories, and keep out all abuses introduced by ignorant professors and others which tended to its degradation.

Let us for one moment pause and endeavour to imagine with what feelings the members of this august body would have beheld in the salon a performance of the "Kitchen Lancers," or on the stage some of those high-kicking acrobatic performances that in our own days pass among the uncultured for dancing !

The example set by Louis XIV. and his court
contributed not a little to elevate and dignify the
dance; but as much, I fear, can scarcely be said
for the example of royalty in modern times.

During the early part of the seventeenth century
it does not seem to have been customary for females
to take part in public or theatrical dances. In the
performance of a ballet called *Le Triomphe de
l'Amour*, Beauchamp — of whom mention has already
been made, and who has been styled "the father
of all dancing masters," from his having formulated
a system of choregraphy and technical instruction—
was accorded the honour of acting as partner to
the King in a minuet. When, however, the same
ballet was afterwards represented at the Odéon, the
female characters were enacted by ladies, and it
was found that this union of the sexes added greatly
to the brilliance of the scene. Some writers aver
that the change was effected by Lully, the composer and arranger of the fêtes; but it has also
been attributed to the repugnance which Beauchamp had to assuming female attire on account
of his strongly-marked features and diminutive
figure.

Be that as it may, women were from this time

considered indispensable for the success of theatrical dancing, and have ever since continued to be the principal support of the ballet.

Among the more famous contemporaries and successors of Beauchamp may be mentioned Blondy, his pupil; Pecour, a celebrated dancer and learned choregraphist; Duport Dauberval; Gardel, to whom the invention of the *menuet de la cour* has been attributed; and Marcel, whose name is also closely connected with that well-known dance.

Of the grand airs assumed by the last-named illustrious teacher many ridiculous stories are current. It has been said, though I certainly do not endorse or even credit the statement, that he imparted no fewer than two hundred and thirty-six different species of bows and courtesies suitable for all occasions; that he often treated his pupils with extreme discourtesy, however high their social rank, exclaiming, "Duchess, you waddle like a duck," or "You courtesy like a dairymaid"; and we are informed that when he grew old, and was tortured with gout, so that he was obliged to descend a staircase backward, he had always with him two valets to lean on instead of using crutches.

Whatever of truth there may be in these state-

ments, it is certain that Marcel became a teacher
of great celebrity. All the fashionable ladies
flocked to his rooms in 1740, when, after passing
before him and bowing according to the rules,
they dropped his fee into a vase placed on a table
for the purpose; and they tolerated his brusque-
ness of manner on account of his great skill. Lord
Chesterfield, in his letters, endeavoured to persuade
his son that the dancing-master would do him more
good than Aristotle, and urged him strongly to take
lessons of Marcel.

There have been other celebrated dancers and
teachers of dancing who certainly have not regarded their own importance, so to speak, through
the diminishing end of the glass. The elder Vestris
declared that the three greatest men in Europe
were himself, Voltaire, and the King of Prussia;
and when, in his old age, he was told that his son
bade fair to surpass him as a dancer, he exclaimed,
with ready wit, "Ah! but then he had Gaëtan
Vestris for his father, an advantage which nature
did not confer upon me."

Apart, however, from the inordinate self-esteem
of the man, there can be no doubt that the dancing
of Gaëtan Vestris, who, notwithstanding the natural

inward tendency of his limbs,* was a perfect model
of the grave style, contributed to bring the art to
an eminent degree of perfection. His grace of
movement was so enchanting that he literally held
his audience spell-bound, and we read that if,
among his admirers, anyone so far forgot himself
as to applaud with his hands while Vestris was
dancing, "an instant check was put to his rapture
by a choral hush."†

Perhaps the greatest improver of the real ballet,
the *ballet d'action*, or that wherein the performer is
both actor and dancer, was J. George Noverre, to
whose writings I alluded in the opening chapter,
and who was called by Garrick the "Shakespeare
of dance." This distinguished man was not only
an expert dancer and composer of ballets, but he
possessed the most lofty ideals concerning his art,
which he set forth in a work remarkable for literary
excellence of style. Since Noverre the best writer
on the subject of ballets has been Carlo Blasis, who
certainly was no *laudator temporis acti*, for he says:
"The dancers of the last century were inferior to

* "*M. Vestris est jarreté, et les gens de l'art ne s'en apper-
cevroient point sans l'entrechat droit, qui le trahit quelquefois.*"
--NOVERRE.

† BURNEY, *History.*

those who flourished towards the latter end of it,
and still more so to those of the beginning of the
present age.   We cannot but admire the perfection
to which modern dancers have brought the art.
They have a much more refined taste than their
predecessors, and their performance is full of gracefulness and charms." *

Whether, since the time of Blasis, the art of
theatrical dancing has developed towards still
greater perfection is a question which I do not
here purpose to discuss.   A history of the modern
ballet would require a volume to itself.   I would
merely remark that, although occasionally high-
class entertainments of this description appear
to meet with a fair amount of success, they are
not, as a rule, appreciated as they should be ; and
a great deal of the dancing that obtains the approbation of modern audiences is in reality dancing
of a very inferior order.   This probably the performers would themselves be the first to admit;
but so long as ability to kick a tambourine held
above the head obtains more applause than is accorded to expression and true gracefulness we can
scarcely expect that ordinary professional dancers

* *Code of Terpsichore*, Part II., chap. vii.

will care to cultivate the higher branches of their art.

And now we will proceed to consider some of those dances of the olden times, which did not require the accessories of stage and machinery. It has been stated that the revival of dancing as a cultivated art dates from the fifteenth century, but it must not be supposed that as a pastime it was not practised during the Middle Ages. As a matter of fact, it had long been regarded as a necessary accomplishment for both sexes, and we find that the heroes of mediæval romances, like the admirable Crichton * of a later century, were generally renowned for their skill in dancing as well as in fighting.

The first dance tune noted by Chappell † dates as far back as "about 1300," and this, we are told, although not wanting in grace, is decidedly "jiggish" in character. Perhaps it was "the music of the minstrels," to which after the

* In a contemporary advertisement printed at Venice in 1580, now in a show-case of the British Museum, it is stated of James Crichton that, in addition to possessing a knowledge of ten languages, of philosophy, theology, mathematics, astrology, the Kabbalah, etc., "he dances excellently."

† *Pop. Music of the Olden Time.*

coronation banquet, the boy-King, Richard II., with the prelates, nobles, knights, and the rest of the company, danced in Westminster Hall.

When Edward III. was married to Philippa, dancing is included among the amusements, which we are told were continued for a space of three weeks. * That it was a fashionable accomplishment in this reign would appear from the fact that the Countess of Salisbury † was the King's partner when the well-known incident occurred which gave rise to that order of knighthood which, according to Selden, "exceeds in majesty, honour, and fame, all chivalrous orders in the world."

The ancient English morris dance, which is supposed to have been of Moorish origin, was probably brought to this country in the reign of Edward III., when John of Gaunt returned from Spain. ‡ The dance appears to have been little better than an absurd species of pantomime, scarcely worthy of notice if it were not for the

---

* See Froissart, also Sir Edward Strachey's " Essay on Chivalry," Int. to Morte d'Arthur.

†   ". . . That fair dame,
     Whose garter slipped down at the famous ball."—
       R. BROWNING, " A Blot on the Scutcheon."

‡ PEEK's *Memoirs of Milton.*

interest which attaches to it on the score of antiquity. In the *Orchesography* of Thoinot Arbeau,* instructions are given for performing the steps of the *Dance des Morisques*, and the author tells us that in his young days it was the custom in good society for a boy to come into the hall when supper was finished, with his face blackened, his forehead bound with white or yellow taffeta, and bells affixed to his legs. The boy then proceeded to dance the Morisque in the manner described. The great feature of the movement was to strike the right and left heels upon the ground alternately twice, and then both heels together, so as to produce a jingling of the bells. This was the ancient and uncorrupted form of the morris dance,† and it has been surmised that the original morris dancers on English soil, who probably represented Moors, and had their faces blackened, were the prototypes of the Ethiopian minstrels of the present day. But it was not

* Published at Langres in 1588.

, † Favine, in his *Theatre of Honour*, mentions a splendid feast given by Gaston de Foix at Vendôme in 1458 when " foure yong laddes and a damosell, attired like savages, daunced an excellent Morisco before the assembly." See also DOUCE's *Illustrations of Shakespeare.*

long before the oriental character of the dance
became subservient to English tradition, and
although the morisco, with his bells, was retained, the chief performers were representatives
of Robin Hood, Maid Marian, and Friar Tuck.
To these were also added a musician, a dysard or
buffoon, and a hobby-horse constructed of wicker-
work, with a pasteboard neck and head. There
is in the churchwardens' books for the year
1537–38 of the parish church of Kingston-upon-
Thames an entry to the effect that there were
retained for the use of morris dancers at Whit-
suntide "a fryer's cote of russet, and a kyrtele
weltyd with red cloth, a Mowren's cote of buckram,
and foure morres-daunsars' cotes of white fustian,
spangelid, and too gryne saten cotes, and disardde's
cote and belles." *

A curious instance of the aversion with which
the morris dancers were regarded by the puri-
tanical in the time of Queen Elizabeth may be
found in Stubbes' *Anatomie of Abuses*, wherein
the writer concludes a long tirade against the
lord of misrule and his accomplices—whom he
politely designates "hell-hounds"—by saying that

* Tyson's *Environs of London.*

if " the fantasticall fooles " who bring them good
things " knewe that as often as they bring anye
to the maintenance of these execrable pastimes
they offer sacrifice to the devill and sathanas, they
would repent and withdraw their hands, which,"
he piously adds, " God graunt they may."

Perhaps the oldest dances of which any actual
descriptions have descended to us were those
known as the " basses danses,"* which, according
to Arbeau, had been discontinued since about 1538,
or fifty years previous to the time at which he wrote
his famous *Dialogue de la Danse.* I am not aware
how many copies of this rare old work are still
extant, but one from which I have made extracts—
perhaps the only one in England—is or was kept
carefully guarded in a show - case of the King's
Library at the British Museum. It is written in
the old French of the sixteenth century. The
author of the work, whose real name was Jehan
Tabouret, was a son of the Bailiff of Dijon, and
was originally intended to succeed his father; but,
in consequence of a vow made by his mother while
he, as a boy, was suffering from a severe illness,

---

* So called because all the steps were performed *terre à terre*, or
close to the ground.

that in the event of his recovery she would dedi-
cate him to the Church, he afterwards became a
priest. Tabouret had always evinced a taste for
dancing, and notwithstanding the sacred nature of
his calling, in which it appears he attained some
eminence, he found ample time to practise and
glean information concerning his favourite art.
In his seventieth year he published, under a *nom
de plume*, the book to which I have already alluded,
and to which I shall frequently have occasion to
refer.

No one could with justice affirm that the instructions given by this illustrious divine to a
hypothetical pupil, whom he facetiously calls
"Capriol," are not sufficiently explicit; indeed, his
opinion of the perspicacity of pupils generally
does not appear to have been of a very flattering
nature. Here, for instance, is a specimen of his
manner of explaining steps. He is informing
"Capriol" how he should advance after saluting
his "damoiselle." Says he, "*vous marcherez en
avant du pied gauche pour la première mesure.
Puis mettrez le pied droit ioinct avec le dict gauche
pour la deuxieme mesure; puis avancerez le pied
droit pour la trosiesme mesure; et à la quatrième*

mesure et battement ioindrez le pied gauche avec le dict pied droit, et ainsisera parfaict le mouvement les deux simples."

Now all this simply means that you are to advance the left foot, then bring the right close against it, after which you advance the right foot and close the left, each movement occupying one measure, and completing what he technically terms two "simples."

I should remark that the "double" of such a movement would be composed of three forward steps, or *pas marchés*, and a closing of the feet at the fourth measure, or count, as we should say, because the writer does not mean that a single step should occupy a whole bar of the music; indeed, much of the music he gives is not divided into bars at all.

It will be noticed that the pupil is advised to commence with the left foot, according to usage; but elsewhere Arbeau informs us that personally he agrees with the opinion held by his master at Poictiers, that it was more correct to begin with the right, since it enabled one to turn his body towards the young lady, "*et lui jetter un gracieux regard.*" The following is a specimen of the music

given by the author for the "*reverence*," or bow
and courtesy, of the partners, with which the
basse danse, like all others of that period, commenced * :—

The dances known as the *branle* and *pavane*,
which were originally connected with the ancient
basse danse, survived it by many generations. The
pavane† was quite popular at the time when
Tabouret wrote his treatise, and he ventured the
opinion that it would never cease to be so. It
is not many years since an attempt was made in
Paris to revive the dance, but it must be confessed
that the modern adaptation did not seem to bear
any particularly striking resemblance to the original
movement.

The music of the pavane was, we are told, frequently played on nuptial occasions, "*quant on
meyne èpouser en face de saincte èglise une fille de
bonne maison.*" The dance was one of a particu-

* In trying these specimens of music, notice should be taken of
the clefs in which they are written.

† From the Latin *pavo*, a peacock.

larly solemn character, as the reader may judge
from the following specimen of music, which is
a reproduction of the original, except that the
minims are round instead of diamond-shaped, the
accidentals before instead of beneath the notes to
which they refer, and the clef-signs modern.

THE PAVANE.

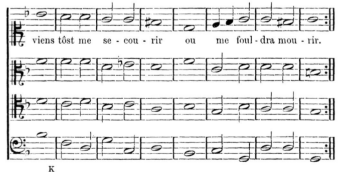

κ

As the reader may find the above music trouble-
some to read, I will rewrite it in the G and F
clefs, so that it may be easily played on a piano.

Anyone who heard the above without being
informed that it was a dance tune, would in all
probability take it for a psalm. But the solemnity
of the music was admirably adapted to the dancers'
movements, which were all of a most grave and
stately character. The pavane was a dance suit-

able for kings, * princes, and peers, who wore during its performance the long robes, gowns, or mantles of their office. The gentlemen carried swords, and the ladies swayed their long trains to and fro upon the ground, so as to resemble the movements of the proud bird from which the dance derived its name.

The dancers in the time of Henry III. of France frequently sang while performing the pavane, and of a suitable *chanson* no fewer than seven verses are given, of which the following will serve as an example, the first verse having already been written beneath the four-part music :—

> "Tes beautés et ta grâce
> Et tes divins propos
> Ont eschauffé la glace
> Qui me gelait les os,
> Et ont remply mon cœur
> D'une amoureuse ardeur.
>
> *   *   *   *
>
> Approche donc, ma belle,
> Approche—toi, mon bien ;
> Ne me sois plus rebelle,
> Puisque mon cœur est tien ;
> Pour mon âme apaiser,
> Donne-moi un baiser."

* Voltaire in his *Siècle de Louis XIV.*, mentions the dance as one in which the young King showed his grace.

There was very little of what may be termed
genuine dancing in the original pavane. There
were two "simple" movements and one "double"
forward, that is a *pas marché* and *assemblé*, or
closing movement, twice alternately with the
left and right foot, then three *pas marchés* and
assemblé. The same could be done *en arrière*, or
backward, beginning with the right foot, or, if
preferred, the movement could always be done *en
avant*. On arriving near the end of the room,
especially if it happened to be at all crowded, it
was proper for the gentleman to go backward,
turning the lady to face him, so that she should
be able to see where she was going; for, as Arbeau
points out, if she went backward with her long
train, she might chance to fall, and then her
partner would probably find himself out of favour.

After having received very explicit instructions
for performing the ancient pavane, the pupil in
Arbeau's "Orchésographie" asks his master if it
does not seem far too grave a dance to perform
with a young girl. To this the teacher replies
that the musicians sometimes play a lighter
measure called a "passemeze," and that a new
kind of pavane has been lately introduced, called

the Pavane d'Espagne, somewhat resembling the Danse des Canaries.* It appears that the commencement of the Spanish pavane did not differ greatly from that of the older French dance, but in the former there followed *coupés, fleurets*, raising of the limbs alternately, and gestures of the body.

The stately pavane was generally succeeded, for the sake of variety, by a particularly light and frisky movement, termed the gaillarde. This appears to have been a sort of "go-as-you-please" dance, the very antithesis of the solemn *terre à terre* movements to which our attention has hitherto been directed. It mattered little what steps you introduced in the "double" so long as you kept time and finished with the foot in a position ready to commence the "simple" by which it was followed. † Thus to raise one foot high from the floor was "*gaillarde*"; to have both feet off the floor was "*encore plus gaillarde*"; but if while making the high leaps the feet were struck together in the air (*capriole*), or crossed and re-

* Spoken of in old English works as the Canary. Sir John Hawkins describes the dance in his *History of Music*, but he probably borrowed from Tabouret.

† "Les bons danceurs agilles et gaillards y peuuent faire tant et tels decoupements et hachures que bon leur semble pourueu qu'ils retumbent à leur cadance." . . .

crossed rapidly (*entrechat*), then it was "gaillarde" in perfection.

It was by his graceful execution of this dance that young Hatton first captivated the heart of Queen Elizabeth. He had been brought up to the law, and entered the court, as his enemy Sir John Perrot used to say, "by the gaillarde," as his first appearance there was on the occasion of a mask ball, and her Majesty was so struck by his good looks and activity that she made him one of her band of pensioners, who were considered the handsomest men in England.* It is said that the favours which the virgin monarch extended to her new favourite excited the jealousy of the whole court, especially that of the Earl of Leicester, who, thinking to depreciate the accomplishments of the young lawyer, offered to introduce to Elizabeth's notice a professional dancer whose saltatory performances were considered far more wonderful than Hatton's. To this suggestion, however, the royal lady, with more vehemence than elegance, exclaimed: "Pish! I will not see your man ; it is his trade."

Thoinot Arbeau gives the actual steps of some

---

* See AGNES STRICKLAND's *Lives of the Queens of England.*

of the gaillardes. Thus the first movement of one,
called "Anthoinette," was composed of four *greues*
alternately with the right and left limbs, then a
"*sault majeur*" and a "*posture gaulche.*" This is
repeated, commencing with the opposite foot, after
which there are further combinations of "*greues*"
postures and "*entretailles.*"

I should explain that the ancient terms *greue*
and *ruade,* expressing forward and backward movements of the limbs in raising the feet, have long
since become obsolete, and even professors of the
art would not understand their application unless
they happened to have made a special study of
antique works.

Although great credit is due to the venerable
Arbeau for the ingenuity he has shown in explaining the dances of his time, he does not, I must
admit, appear to have been particularly fortunate
in the selection of his melodies. Most of these
are distinctly religious in character, and some
would seem to be altogether ill suited to the movements for which they are intended. Here, for
instance, is a "gaillarde"!

The name of this dismal tune is appropriate
enough, "*La traditore my fa mourire.*" Of course
the music might be played as if written in ⅜ time,
but it would never sound gay. Most of the
gaillardes given by Arbeau are equally melancholy.
Here, however, are the first eight bars of a better
specimen from Chappell's *Music of the Olden Time.*
It is called—

"GAILLARDE SWEET MARGARET." *

The above music was frequently used for the
famous kissing dance "Joan Saunderson," which did

* "The earliest printed copy I have found," says Chappell, "is
in the *Tablature de Luth intitulé* '*Le Secret des Muses*' (4to, Am-
sterdam, 1615), where it is called 'Gaillarde Anglaise.'"

not generally terminate until each lady of the party had been kissed twice by all the men, and each man twice by all the ladies. This interesting dance was admirably calculated to banish all feelings of reserve from social gatherings. A ring of male and female dancers, placed alternately, was formed, and one of the men, taking a cushion in his hand, danced round the inside thereof till the end of the tune. Then he suddenly stopped, and began to sing, "This dance it will no further go," whereupon the musicians demanded, "I pray you, good sir, why say you so?" and to this he replied, "Because Joan Saunderson will not come to, and she must come to whether she will or no." He then laid the cushion at the feet of one of the ladies, and on this she had to kneel down to receive the salutation. It is true that at first the girl selected generally made some show of reluctance to comply, but no sooner had the osculatory process been gone through than she evinced a considerable degree of satisfaction, for she got up, according to the rules, and danced round with the man, singing, "Prinkum prankum is a fine dance, and shall we go dance it over again?" When it was the lady's turn to carry the cushion she placed it at the feet of one

of the men, and as she received the kiss sang,
"Welcome, John Saunderson; welcome, welcome!"

For the cushion dance, above described, the following bars were added to the graver melody, their
English character being unmistakable:—

In many of the old-time dances it was customary
to commence operations by kissing one's partner;
indeed, if one neglected to take the opportunity
afforded, it would have appeared as great a breach
of etiquette as it would if, at a later date, one had
neglected to make the prescribed bow in commencing
a quadrille.   Thus, in Shakespeare's *Henry VIII.*,*

* Act I., scene iv.

the King, when he dances with Anne Bullen, says:

> "Sweetheart,
> I were unmannerly to take you out,
> And not to kiss you."

From a verse of Steevens'[*] it would appear that the gentleman was entitled to salute the lady in like manner on finishing the dance, a privilege which is sarcastically put forward as its chief attraction:—

> . . . "What fool would dance
> If that, when dance is done,
> He may not have at lady's lips
> That which in dance he won?"

The ancient gavotte was a dance of this description. Arbeau, in describing how it was performed more than three hundred years ago, says: "*Quand les dits danceurs ont quelque peu dancé l'un d'iceulx (avec sa damoiselle), s'escarté à part, et fait quelques passages au meillieu de la dance au conspect de tous les aultres, puis il vient baiser toutes les aultres damoiselles, et sa damoiselle tous les aultres hommes, et puis se remettent en leur renc; ce fait, le second danceur en fait aultant, et consequemment tous les aultres.*" The steps of this genial dance were of a sprightly nature, like those of the gaillarde.

---

[*] Quoted by Southey in his *Original Memoranda*.

The coranto, which, it will be remembered, was
the dance that Claude Duval compelled the lady
to perform with him upon the heath, was also of
a lively character, most of the steps being jumped.
Originally it was danced in the form of a ballet.
Three young men selected partners, and placed
themselves in order. The first dancer then led
his lady to the other end of the room, and returned
alone to his companions; the second did likewise,
and then the third, so that the three ladies were
separated from their partners. The first gentleman
then approached his lady with light steps, making
signs as if courting her regard, nicely adjusting his
garments,* and assuming an air of tenderness.
The lady, however, was generally inconsiderate
enough to reject these advances, and even to turn
her back upon her lover, who thereupon returned
to his place with gesticulations of despair. The
two other gentlemen then approached their partners
in turn, and with a similar result. But not to
be daunted by a repulse, seeing that "faint heart
ne'er won fair lady," the three gallants determined
to make a final effort, and on the principle, I sup-

---

* "*Espoussetant ses chausses, tirant sa chemise bien à propos.*"
—TABOURET.

pose, that "unity is strength," they went forward
this time together, with hands joined, and kneeling
each before his lady, they pleaded for mercy. This
combined appeal the fair ones were unable to
resist; they surrendered themselves to the arms
of their admirers, and proceeded to dance the
coranto pell-mell.*

I notice that, in explaining the movements of the
courante to his pupil, Arbeau remarks that the
young men of his day would not always trouble
to learn the proper steps of a dance. This peculiarity has been by no means confined to the male
dancers of the sixteenth century. Allusion is made
by Plato to a tendency amongst the young Greeks
to disregard the rules of dancing, and the great
philosopher is justly severe on such delinquents,
for, as we have seen, he was himself an admirer
of the art. Doubtless there were Spartan youths
who imagined that any kind of steps would do for
the ὅρμος so long as they contrived to meet their
partner at the right juncture, just as there are
young men of the present time—and these not
a few—who appear to think that any kind of

* "*Sois les dictes damoiselles se rendoient entre leurs bras et
dancoient la dite courante pesle mesle.*"—*Ibid.*

undignified shuffle will do for a waltz so long as
one manages to get round in time with the music.
Human nature has been much the same in all ages.
On one occasion "Capriol," in the *Orchesography,*
asks if he may not lead out two "damoiselles"
instead of one, and to this his master, with the
experience of riper years, replies that he may do
so if he likes, but in his opinion one lady at a
time is quite sufficient. "*Trop en ha qui deux en
meine,*" says he, quoting an ancient proverb.

At one time, during the reign of Charles II., the
coranto appears to have occupied much the same
position in English ball-rooms as the waltz does at
the present day, if we may trust an entry made
by Samuel Pepys in his *Diary,* in which the author
complains that at a court ball given on the 15th
of November, 1666, there was so little variety in
the dances that "the courants grew tiresome." The
dancing on another occasion, when Pepys was present, at Whitehall, and to which I shall shortly
refer, appears to have been of a far more enjoyable
and varied nature.

The branle, to which allusion has already been
made, was a grave *terre à terre* dance, and received
its name from a swaying motion of the limbs.

Generally it was danced by couples in the same manner as the pavane; but in some branles, as, for instance, in the *Branle de Malte*, the dancers were placed in a ring. In England the dance, which was popular during the sixteenth and part of the seventeenth centuries, and especially at the court of Elizabeth, has been frequently spoken of as the "brawl." The poet Gray says :—

> "Full oft within the spacious walls,
> When he had fifty winters o'er him,
> My grave Lord Keeper led the brawls ;
> The seals and maces danced before him."

The volta, or "the lavolta," as it is sometimes ungrammatically called in old books,* is a dance to which special interest attaches, as being the prototype of the modern waltz. The volta, as its name implies, was of Italian origin, and has been described as a dance in which "the man turns the woman round several times, and then assists her to make the high spring or cabriole." Shakespeare, in *Henry V.*, says :—

> "They bid us to the English dancing schools,
> And teach lavoltas high and swift corantos";

---

* The foreign article should properly be omitted when the English one is used. To say *the lavolta* is, strictly speaking, as incorrect as to say *the la polka*.

and Sir John Davis, in his poem called "The
Orchestra," alludes to the dance thus:—

> "Yet is there one, the most delightful kind,
>   A lofty jumping or a leaping round,
>   Where arm in arm two dancers are entwined,
>   And where, themselves in strict embracements bound,
>   An anapæst is all their music's song,
>   Whose first two feet are short and third is long."

The following is the air of a volta as given by
Thoinot Arbeau:—

This, written in the modern style, would appear
as below; but the melody, like many others selected
by the good old Canon, is by no means remarkable
for its beauty.

Without doubt, and seemingly with good reason,
the introduction of the volta met with considerable
opposition. M. Bodin, a writer on demonology,
averred that its importation into France had been
effected by the power of witches; and John North-
brooke, author of *A Treatise against Dauncing*,

after expressing general disapprobation of the practice, ventures the opinion that the women must have invented round dances "so that, holding upon men's arms, they might hop the higher."* Even Arbeau himself disapproves of the volta, for, after giving explicit directions as to how the gentleman should assist his partner to perform the great leap, and how the lady should conduct herself as decorously as possible in the circumstances—directions, by the way, which, amusing as they are, it would scarcely be advisable to reproduce—he proceeds to say : " *Ce fait, vous ferez par ensemble les tours de la volte, comme ç'y dessus a esté dit ; et, après avoir tournoyé par tant de cadance qu'il vous plaira, restituerez la damoiselle en sa place, ou elle sentira (quelque bonne continence qu'elle face) son cerveau esbranlé, plein de vertigues et tornoyements de tête, et vous n'en aurez peult estre pas moins. Je vous laisse à considerer si c'est chose bien seant à une jeusne fille de faire de grands pas ouvertures de iambes. Et si en ceste volte l'honneur et la santé y sont pas hazardez et interessez, je vous en ay désia dit mon opinion.*"

* Other pious authors have expressed particular aversion to high steps. For instance, John Chrysostom (Homily XLIX., I think) assures us that " feet were not given to us for dancing, but to walk modestly, not to leap impudently, like camels."

L

No wonder, then, that the good folks were
scandalised when Mary Stuart exhibited her
agility in the volta, although, as the Scotch
ambassador declared, she "dancit not so hich and
so disposedly" as did her royal cousin of
England! *

It would seem that after the time of Elizabeth
the practice of dancing in this country began to
degenerate. In the *Table Talk of John Selden*,
compiled by Milward, and first published in 1689,
some years after his death, we find the following
remarks: "The court of England is much altered.
At a solemn dancing, first you had the grave
measure, then the coranto and the galliard, and
this kept up with the ceremony, and at length
the trenchmore and the cushion dance, then all
the company dances, lord and groom, lady and
kitchenmaid, no distinction. So in our court in
Queen Elizabeth's time gravity of state was kept
up. In King James' time things were pretty well.
But in King Charles' time there has been nothing
but trenchmore and the cushion dance, omnium
gatherum, tolly-polly, hoite cum toite."

The cushion dance I have already described.

* MELVILLE'S *Memoirs*.

Trenchmore was danced in a line, the men facing their partners. In commencing, all led forward and back three times; then the dancers "cast off" to the right and left, met below, and came up the centre. This they also did three times, after which the first couple went down under the arms of the second couple, while the third couple came up under their arms. There were other figures, but the above will suffice to give an idea of the dance. The music of trenchmore began as follows:—

In the original description of trenchmore there are no instructions about kissing the ladies; but the famous old dance known as "All in a Garden Green" appears to have been one of a particularly cordial nature. Six dancers placed themselves lengthways, and after the usual "lead up all a double, forward and back," proceeded as follows (I will give the instructions exactly as they appear

in the *Dancing Master* of 1665): "First man shake
his own wo:* by the hand, then the 2†, then the
3‡ by one hand, then by the other, kisse her twice,
turn her, shake her by the hand, then the 2, then
your own by one hand, then by the other, kisse her
twice, and turn her," etc.

It will be noticed that the personal pronouns
and general directions are a little mixed in the
above description; but it is sufficiently clear to
show that "All in a Garden Green" must have
been a very jolly dance. Pressure of space will
only permit me to give the first eight bars of the
lovely melody by which it was accompanied.§

* Woman.
† Second.
‡ Third.
§ Chappell gives this melody in the key of F. He says, "By
registration of Sta. Co., we find that in 1565 William Pickering
had a licence to print a Ballett intitulled all in a garden grene,
between two lovers."

Among the oldest English dances of which
we have any authentic description was one called
"Dargerson," which was popular in the reign of
Henry VII. In this the dancers did not face each
other, as in the contra-dance,* nor did they form a
ring, but placed themselves all in a continuous line.
For example, if there were eight people dancing
they would, in commencing, stand thus:—

M. M. M. M. W. W. W. W.

the M.'s representing the men and the W.'s the
women. This arrangement seems to obviate the
necessity of selecting partners, because all dance

---

* Chappell is of opinion that our term "country dance" is not
derived from the French contre-danse, as is generally supposed,
and he supports his argument by stating that in many of the
so-called country dances the couples did not stand facing one
another at all. He points out also that the French etymologists
have reversed the position. Thus in the *Ency. Methodique* "*ce
mot*" (*contredanse*) "*paroît venir de l'Anglois, country dance—danse
de compagne*," etc.

together by turns. It will be apparent that if the
first man set to and turned with the woman nearest
to him, so that they changed places, and then they
each set to and turned with the next dancer, and
so on, the position of the men and women would
after a certain number of turns have been reversed,
and they would all have danced together once.
Then they returned in the same manner to their
places. After this they linked arms "as they
sided," and then performed the "hey," or chain,
giving hands as they passed till they came again
to their original places.

Many people think that square dances, as they
are called, are of comparatively modern invention
and French origin; but, as a matter of fact, they
were known in England three hundred years ago.
"Dull Sir John" and "Faine I Would" were both
dances in which four couples stood facing each
other, as they now do in the Quadrille and Lancers,
only with this difference: the lady stood on the
left-hand side of her partner instead of on his
right.

We have seen that, according to Selden, dancing
degenerated after the reign of Elizabeth, but in
the time of Charles II. it appears to have been

practised and appreciated to a considerable extent. Count Lorenzo Magalotte, who visited England in 1669 with the Grand Duke of Tuscany, describes how the dancing schools of London were frequented both by married and unmarried ladies, "who," says he, "are instructed by the master, and practise with much gracefulness and agility various dances after the English fashion." * He also adds : " Dancing is a very common and favourite amusement of the ladies in this country; every evening there are entertainments at different places in the city, at which many ladies and citizens' wives are present, they going to them alone, as they do to the rooms of the dancing masters, at which there are frequently upwards of forty or fifty ladies. His Highness had an opportunity of seeing several dances in the English style exceeding well regulated, and executed in the smartest and genteelest manner by very young ladies, whose beauty and gracefulness were shown off to perfection in this exercise." Count Lorenzo was evidently a man of discernment, and his concluding phrase should be well digested by mothers into whose hands this volume may chance to fall.

* *Harl. Mis.*, vol. vii.

A few pages back, when treating of the coranto,
I referred to the diary of Samuel Pepys. The
following extract from the same work will doubtless prove interesting to the reader who desires
information respecting dancing as it was practised
at the court of the gay monarch. Writing in 1662,
the author says :—

"Mr. Povy and I to White Hall, he taking
me thither on purpose to carry me into the ball
this night before the King. He brought me first
to the Duke's chamber, where I saw him and
the Duchess at supper, and thence into the room
where the ball was to be, crammed with fine
ladies, the greatest of the court. By-and-by comes
the King and Queen, the Duke and Duchess, and
all the great ones; and after seating themselves
the King takes out the Duchess of York, and the
Duke the Duchess of Buckingham, the Duke of
Monmouth my Lady Castlemaine, and so other
lords other ladies, and they danced the Brantle.
After that the King led a lady a single coranto, and
then the rest of the lords, one after another, other
ladies; very noble it was, and great pleasure to see.
Then to country dances, the King leading the first,
which he called for, which was, says he, 'Cuckolds

all Awry,' the old dance of England. Of the ladies
that danced, the Duke of Monmouth's mistress, and
my Lady Castlemaine, and a daughter of Sir Harry
de Vicke's were the best. The manner was, when
the King dances, all the ladies in the room, and
the Queen herself, stand up; and, indeed, he dances
rarely, and much better than the Duke of York.
Having staid there as long as I thought fit, to my
infinite content, it being the greatest pleasure I
could wish now to see at court, I went home,
leaving them dancing."

Referring to the dance, with the somewhat in-
elegant name, which Charles II. described as the
"old dance of England," I observe that in the
Dancing Master of that period the unfortunate
individuals are represented as being "all arow,"
not "all awry," and in Chappell's *Popular Music
of the Olden Time* the tune is given as "Cuckolds
all a Row." Anyhow here is the quaint old music,
which I will take from the last-mentioned work :—

Many of the names of the old English dances
are, to say the least, peculiar, and some few would
be positively unmentionable to modern polite ears,
so that if the dances were ever revived they would
certainly have to be rechristened. Our ancestors
possessed very little notion of what is termed
"rosewater morality," and they had no scruple
whatever about calling a useful garden implement
by its proper name.

I am not, of course, going to give instances of
titles of dances that would not bear repetition;
but confining our attention only to peculiar ones,
imagine how strange it would sound if at a ball
the steward were to say, "Now, gentlemen, take
your partners for 'Lumps of Pudding,'" for "Under
and Over," for "The Bath," or for "Up Tails All."
Yet each of these was once a well-known dance.
The country dances were generally called by the
names of the tunes which accompanied them, and

some of these were singularly unenticing to the
ear. Take, for example, "The Slaughterhouse"
—what a name for a dance!—"An Old Man a
Bed full of Bones," "Rub her down with Straw,"
"Have at thy Coat, Old Woman," or "The Ladies'
Misfortune." Surely it is a wonder that dances
with such titles could ever have become popular.

Among the dances with pleasanter names I
may mention "The Happy Marriage"—this by way
of contrast to Charles the Second's characteristic
"Old Dance of England"—"Dissembling Love," for
three couples; "Sweet Kate," a dance for an
unlimited number, in which there was clapping of
hands and holding up of fingers; "The Maids'
Morris," a simple pleasing dance; "Once I Loved
a Maiden Fair"; and "Green Sleeves."

"The Triumph," a dance in which two men join
their hands to form an arch above the lady's head,
is still, I believe, occasionally seen at country
houses, and "Sir Roger de Coverley," or "The Slip,"
as it was originally called, seems to enjoy perennial
popularity. Most of the others mentioned have long
since been forgotten, and the figures are only known
to those who care to study and work them out from
old books in which descriptions may be found.

A dance in which, according to the instructions given, the first man in commencing "casts off, goes up to the third woman, kisses her, and returns to his place," was called "The Last New Vagaries." It would scarcely do to introduce such "vagaries" into dancing nowadays; but they were apparently quite popular in the reign of Queen Anne.

Perhaps the following contemporary sketch of a dancing academy at this period may prove interesting to the reader. Budgell (*Spectator*) says: "I am a man in years, and by an honest industry in the world have acquired enough to give my children a liberal education, though I was an utter stranger to it myself. My eldest daughter, a girl of sixteen, has for some time past been under the tuition of Monsieur Rigadoon, a dancing-master in the city; and I was prevailed upon by her and her mother to go last night to one of his balls. I must own to you, sir, that, having never been at any such place before, I was very much pleased and surprised with that part of his entertainment which he called *French dancing*. There were several young men and women whose limbs seemed to have no other motion but purely what the music gave them. After this part was over they began a diversion

which they call *country dáncing,* and wherein there
were also some things not disagreeable, and divers
emblematical figures, composed, as I guess, by wise
men for the instruction of youth.

"Amongst the rest I observed one, which I think
they call 'Hunt the Squirrel,' in which the woman
flies and the man pursues her; but as soon as she
turns he runs away, and she is obliged to follow.

"The moral of this dance does, I think, very
aptly recommend modesty and discretion in the
female sex.

"But as the best institutions are liable to corruption, so, sir, I must acquaint you that very
great abuses are crept into this entertainment. I
was amazed to see my girl handed by and handing
young fellows with so much familiarity, and I
could not have thought it had been my child.
They very often made use of a most impudent
and lascivious step called *setting* to partners, which
I know not how to describe to you but by telling
you that it is the very reverse of *back to back.* At
last an impudent young dog bid the fiddlers play
a dance called *Moll Patley,* and, after having made
two or three capers, ran to his partner, locked his
arms in hers, and whisked her round cleverly above

ground in such a manner that I, who sat upon one
of the lowest benches, saw further above her.shoe
than I can think fit to acquaint you with. I could
no longer endure these enormities, wherefore, just
as my girl was going to be made a whirligig, I
ran in, seized my child, and carried her home."

In addition to the country dances and jigs, of
which, as I have already hinted, there was an
infinite variety, foreign dances were also popular
in England at this period, such, for instance, as
the rigaudon, a dance of Provençal origin, the
solemn louvre, and stately minuet.

The last-mentioned dance will be treated of more
particularly in my next chapter. Its origin has
never, I believe, been satisfactorily settled, though
it is said to have come from Poitou, and to derive
its name from the neat character of the steps employed. It is probably a more ancient dance than
is generally supposed, for it is stated that Don Juan
of Austria travelled *incog.* from Brussels to Paris
in order to see Marguerite de Valois, who was
considered one of the best dancers of her day,
"walk a minuet" at a ball. The earliest known
minuet music was composed by Lully, in 1663,
for Louis XIV. ; but possibly the minuet, in a

rustic form, was danced by the peasants of Anjou ages before it reached the monarch's court.

It has been suggested, and not without some show of reason, that the stately, solemn, and formal dances of the eighteenth century were not necessarily adopted through grave inclination or ceremonious respect, but were the natural outcome of the prevailing style of dress. The high-heeled shoes and enormous hoops worn by the ladies were by no means favourable to rapidity of movement; and any attempt at jumping steps would soon have involved the elaborately piled-up structures of powdered hair and ornament, by which their heads were adorned (or disfigured), in hopeless ruin.

The quadrille and the waltz were introduced into England at about the same time. Raikes gives the date of the latter event as 1813, and declares that none other ever produced so great a sensation in English society. He relates how the mornings, which had hitherto been dedicated to lounging in the park, were now "absorbed at home in practising the figures of a French quadrille, or whirling a chair round the room to learn the step and measure of the German waltz." The author moralises upon the scenes he had witnessed in those days at

Almack's: "What fear and trembling in the *débu-
tantes* at the commencement of a waltz, what giddi-
ness and confusion at the end!" which, by the
way, is very much like what had been said concerning the volta by old Jehan Tabouret more than two
centuries previously.

Referring to the opposition which was at first
directed against the waltz, Raikes adds: "The
anti-waltzing party took the alarm, cried it down,
mothers forbade it, and every ball-room became a
scene of feud and contention; the waltzers continued their operations, but their ranks were not
filled with so many recruits as they expected. The
foreigners, however, were not idle in forming their
élèves. Baron Tripp, Newmann, St. Aldegonde, etc.,
persevered in spite of all the prejudices which were
marshalled against them. Every night the waltz
was called, and new votaries, though slowly, were
added to their train. Still the opposition party did
not relax their efforts, sarcastic remarks flew about,
and pasquinades were written to deter young ladies
from such a recreation.

"The waltz, however," continues the author of
the journal, "struggled successfully through all its
difficulties; Flahault, who was *la fleur du pois* in

Paris, came over to captivate Miss Mercer, and, with a host of others, drove the prudes into their entrenchments. And when the Emperor Alexander was seen waltzing round the room at Almack's, with his tight uniform and numerous decorations, they surrendered at discretion."

The figures of the quadrille, when first imported into this country, were materially different from those with which we are acquainted. Originally the dance was executed by four persons only, but shortly afterwards four more were added to complete the square. Being formed on the plan of the old country dances (which had been taught in France by an English professor a hundred years previously, but had not become popular until Rameau introduced one in his " Fêtes de Polymnie "), the actions of clapping the hands and menacing with the fingers were admitted, as in " Sweet Kate," a dance to which I have already alluded. Soon, however, new figures were added, but they were all danced with more or less difficult steps, such as are used in gavottes ; in fact, the figure known as *Trenis* was actually taken from a gavotte of the period which had been introduced in a ballet, and had become a general favourite.

M

The author of *Memoirs of the Times of George IV.*
considered the practice of "quadrilling" as then
newly exhibited in England* "very abominable."
He admits that he is not prude enough to be
offended with waltzing, in which, he says, he "can
see no other harm than that it disorders the
stomach, and sometimes makes people look very
ridiculous"—observations which, judging from old
plates and descriptions such as those given by
Wilson, Blasis, and others, of the waltz as it was
originally danced, were, I should say, perfectly
justified. "But the quadrilles," continues our
author, "I can by no means endure, for till
ladies and gentlemen have joints at their ankles,
which is impossible, it is worse than impudent
to make such exhibitions"; and then he wisely
adds, "When people dance to be looked at, they
surely should dance to perfection."

The waltz and quadrille are by far the oldest
dances which are now at all generally practised
in our ball-rooms. The latter, it must be candidly
admitted, can no longer be regarded as a favourite;
but the former at least appears to have lost nothing
of its extraordinary popularity—a popularity which,

* That is, in 1811.

as I have elsewhere endeavoured to show in practically considering the dance,* is mainly dependent
upon the fact that the movements employed in
waltzing, when waltzing is perfect, are admirably
in accordance with the natural mechanism of the
human frame. Meanwhile, having taken a rapid
survey of the ancient practice of dancing, and
having more or less briefly considered the principal
dances that have obtained popularity from the far-
off times, when the Pharaohs sat upon the throne
of Egypt, to the introduction of the most remarkable dance of modern days, let us, before turning
our attention to the present degenerate condition
of the art, pause awhile to examine the true nature
of that "queen of dances" which was the delight
of our more immediate ancestors.

* *Dancing*, All England Series.

CHAPTER VII.

THE MINUET.

IF an article treating of ancient dances is to be accounted of any real value, it ought to be supported by the most undeniable authority. The names of Pecour, Gardel, Rameau, and Marcel are those most immediately associated with the elaboration and detail of the celebrated dance which we are about to consider, and it is on the teaching and opinions of these men that I intend to base my present observations. At the same time, as already hinted in my last chapter, it must not be supposed that the minuet originated at the French court, or that it was the invention of any of the above-named teachers. To them the minuet doubtless owes much of its elegance and refinement; but as a rustic dance it was probably known to the peasants of Anjou ages before it became the pastime of kings and princes.

There seems to be a somewhat general impression

that the court minuet was a particularly stagey
dance, so to speak, in which there was a great deal
of affected attitudinising, and that during its performance the partners were continually bowing and
courtesying to one another. This impression is,
however, a mistaken one. It is true that Magri
considered a "languishing eye and a smiling mouth"
indispensable accessories to the minuet; but surely
it would not appear becoming for dancers to look
sorrowful; and as to the languishing eye, well,
do we never see it during the performance of a
waltz? Probably this was only an Italian's way
of suggesting that the partners should look pleasant,
and not appear as if they were bored with each
other's company. An affected manner of dancing
the minuet was distinctly to be avoided, according
to Rameau, who says in his instructions, "*mais
surtout sans affectation*," and, so far as the bows
and courtesies are concerned, there was a double
salutation at the beginning of the dance, occupying
eight measures, and a similar one at the finish;
that was all.

Most people naturally derive their ideas of the
minuet from representations they may have seen
on the stage. But we should remember that in

such representations the chief object which the
arranger has in view is the gratification of the
audience, and consequently he will be often
tempted to introduce effects which, although
pleasing in themselves, do not properly belong to
the dance in question. The couples diverge to the
right and left, and arrange their movements so
that they may continually face the audience. The
ladies sometimes cross before the gentlemen; then
they make *demi-tours de mains*, and bow and
courtesy repeatedly throughout the dance. The
ladies go to the centre, spread out their fans, and
move round in one direction, while their partners
promenade the opposite way. These devices are
now often used indiscriminately in stage minuets
and gavottes, as they are called, the difference
between the two dances being more discernible
in the music than in their manner of execution.

This, however, is not quite as it should be.
The gavotte, it is true, is a dance which admits
of considerable latitude. The original dance of
the gavots was, as we have already seen, a rustic
kissing dance, and the kissing privilege was by
no means neglected when it became popular in
the higher ranks of society. The famous gavotte

introduced by Vestris was a dance of a very different order, consisting of *ailes de pigeons, entrechats*, and all kinds of difficult steps and elaborate *enchaînements*, such as can only be properly executed by an experienced dancer. There have been gavottes innumerable. The fourth figure of the quadrille was taken from one. A gavotte may be arranged with or without difficult steps. I have seen one performed almost entirely with the *pas de basque*, which, being well executed, did not look at all amiss; but, generally speaking, the steps employed in a gavotte should be of a livelier nature than those of the minuet, which is a solemn *terre-à-terre* dance, and the movements should have a distinct character.

Various minuets have also been arranged from time to time. To mention a few only, there were the *Menuet de la Cour*, the *Menuet de la Reine*, the *Menuet d'Exaudet*, the *Menuet Dauphin*, and the Rose-coloured Minuet, which the young princess, greatly to the disgust of her dancing-master, insisted should be renamed the " Blue Minuet." *

Lully, in the seventeenth century, arranged music for court minuets, and later there have been the

* *Vide* Madame CAMPAN's *Memoirs of Marie Antoinette.*

minuet from "Iphigenie," by Gluck, the minuets
from "Titus" and "Don Juan," by Mozart, the
minuets of Bocherini, and many others, all of
which have been composed expressly for dancing.

To anyone who understands how motion should
be wedded to music, it will be evident that an
arrangement of steps and figures suitable for some
of these compositions would not be at all well
adapted for others; yet we know that they have
all been danced to, and most of us have seen the
minuet in Don Juan performed at the opera. As
a matter of fact, this is one of the easiest minuet
compositions, since each part of the tune consists
of eight measures; but at the same time it is not
suitable for the *menuet de la Cour*, because the
principal figure of that classic dance occupies twelve
measures of the music, and although by repetition
of the figure the movements of the dancers are
again brought into accord with the melody, such
an arrangement seems scarcely satisfactory in an
artistic sense. The "Don Juan" minuet is well
marked, and, like the minuet in "Iphigenie," and
some of those by Handel, lends itself to an easy
combination of figures.

It must not be supposed that I wish in any way

to disparage the stage devices to which I drew
attention a few paragraphs back. On the contrary,
some of them are extremely pretty, especially those
in which the arms are interlaced, and which, properly speaking, belong to the *allemande* rather than
the minuet. But although some of the movements
indicated may be used with good effect in *show
dances* of the minuet order, I would suggest that
they do not comprise what is known as the *Menuet
de la Cour*. If anyone would undertake to teach
that time-honoured production, let him be careful
to teach it as nearly as possible in its original form.

I say as *nearly as possible* in its original form,
because it is a very difficult matter to decide between conflicting authorities as to which is likely
to be the most accurate. It is only the ignorant
who are cocksure about such matters. There exist,
we know, teachers of dancing who will undertake
to impart *the* minuet, as if only one form of the
dance had ever been in use, and that form had
never been altered. In nine cases out of ten it
happens that such teachers have taken their minuet
on trust from some other teacher, who possesses as
little knowledge of the history and traditions of
the dance as they do themselves. However, being

acquainted with only one form of the minuet, they
think it impossible that what they do know can be
other than perfect, and in a sense they remind one
of those good old country folks who, having never
left their native village, are apt to conceive a decided opinion that the particular place where they
dwell is the loveliest spot in the world.

For my own part, although I have consulted
many authorities, both ancient and modern, and
have searched in all available sources for information concerning the evolution of the minuet, it is
with the greatest diffidence that I venture to express
opinions on the subject. And this diffidence the
reader will perceive to be only natural and proper
in a modern writer when he learns that the distinguished Marcel, who taught the dance when it
was at the zenith of its popularity, was nevertheless
known to observe in his old age that, although he
had been studying the graces of the minuet all his
life, he had still much to learn. *Que de choses dans
un menuet!* exclaimed this renowned teacher on
another occasion; and indeed it is scarcely to be
wondered at that he should have been somewhat
enthusiastic about a dance by the teaching of which
he had amassed a considerable fortune.

But although authorities may differ with regard to detail, although during its century of popularity the minuet doubtless underwent considerable change, although the original simple figures were added to, and the movements elaborated from time to time, there are some points about which there can be no question, about which all genuine authorities are agreed. These I will present at once to my readers, in order that they may discover if the particular dance which has been shown or imparted to them as the *Menuet de la Cour* has any pretensions whatever to archæological correctness.

First. In the *Menuet de la Cour* there were only two salutations, one at the beginning and one at the end of the dance. Each salutation consisted of two bows, and occupied in all eight measures of the music.

Second. The track of each dancer in performing the *figure principale* took the form of the letter Z.

Third. All minuet steps (*pas de menuet*), whether taken forward, to the right, to the left, or in turning, invariably began with the right foot, both for the lady and the gentleman.

Fourth. All real *pas de menuet* occupied two

measures of the music, and in executing them
the balance of the body was transferred from one
limb to the other only four times.

No one who is acquainted with the true theory
and history of the minuet will question the accuracy
of the above statements; but the casual reader,
who has not gone deeply into the subject, may
convince himself that they are correct by studying
Rameau's *Maître à Danser*, published in 1725, and
other contemporary works. Should the reader be
unable to obtain old books on dancing—and at
the present time they are very rare—he will find
what is here said concerning the steps of the
minuet verified in Coulon's little handbook, which
contains a somewhat elaborate version of the
Menuet de la Cour. In this version many more
steps and figures are introduced than belonged to
the original dance, and the description thereof is
not particularly lucid; but the reader will perceive
that there are only two salutations, one at the
beginning and one at the end. A description of
the correct minuet step *en avant* may also be found
in Peacock's *Sketches*, published in 1805; but the
book is less readily procurable.

M. Desrats, in his *Traité de la Danse*, has given

a simplified version of steps and figures of the
minuet, which he describes as being *plus à la portée
de nos danseurs;* and M. de Soria has arranged a
dance which he calls *Menuet de Louis XV.* The
name, however, is not quite appropriate, seeing
that it bears but little resemblance to the minuet
of that period. Perhaps one of the most correct
versions of the dance to be found in any modern
work is that given in Zorn's *Grammar of Dancing.*

In minuet music, which should always be played
slowly and majestically, there is generally a decided
accent on the note occupying the second interval
of the bar, as well as on the first and third. This
peculiarity gives the minuet rhythm an entirely
different character from that of the waltz, however
slowly the music of the latter dance may be played.
There are other distinguishing features in minuet
composition, but these belong rather to the domain
of music than of dancing.

The minuet, according to Ménage, derives its
name from the word *menu,* signifying little, neat,
this being the manner in which the steps of the
dance should be made.

According to genuine authorities, the following
are the different *pas de menuet,* which, as previously

stated, all occupy two measures of the music or six counts :—

STEPS OF THE MINUET.

1. *Forward Step* (*Pas de menuet en avant*). Suppose the right foot to be in the *second* or *fourth rearward position* * (this being regulated by the previous movement) and the balance of the body sustained on the left limb. At the first count begin to advance the right foot, and as it comes into the *first position* in passing the supporting limb make a decided *plié*, bending the knees outward. At the second count step lightly on the right foot, and commence to advance the left foot, again making a *plié de genoux* as soon as it comes against the right in the *first position*, but without transfer of balance. This completes the first measure of the music. At the first count of the next bar the left foot is put down, and two simple steps follow, forming a *pas de bourrée* of three movements, the balance of the body being supported on the left leg previous to recommencing the step.

N.B.—When the step is executed a second time in turning to face one's partner, the right foot, at the fifth count, is crossed before the left to enable one to turn half round on both toes.

2. *Minuet Step to the Right* (*Pas de menuet à droite*). Starting say from the fifth position, let the right toe

---

* It is assumed that the reader is acquainted with the rudiments of dancing. For technical explanations reference may be made to my double volume in the All England Series of Handbooks.

glide into the *second position*, the distance between the feet being small. Then transfer the balance of the body to the right leg, and bring the left foot slowly to the rearward *fifth position*.* This occupies the first measure. For the second measure transfer the balance of the body to the left leg, slide the right foot again to the *second position*, and bring the left to the *fifth position*, finishing with the balance thereon.

Minuet Step to the Left (Pas de menuet à gauche). Commence by stepping a little forward with the right foot, and in doing so make a decided *plié* with the left knee. Now bring the left foot up to the *first position*, and with a flexion of the knees commence to move it towards the *second position*. This finishes the first measure. For the second bar put the left foot down in the *second position* with transfer of balance to the left leg, draw the right foot slowly to the rearward *fifth position*, and again extend the left to the *second position*, finishing with the balance supported thereon.

N.B.—In repeating this *pas de menuet* to the left, commence by stepping a little backward instead of forward with the right foot; then bring the left to the *first position* with a flexion of the knees, after which proceed as already described.

---

* Sometimes one sees the heel brought to the toe in front ; but few amateur dancers can turn out their feet sufficiently to render the movement effective.

The order of figures in the minuet, as arranged by Pecour, and transmitted to us by Rameau and other authorities, is as follows:—

PRACTICAL DESCRIPTION OF THE DANCE.

During the first eight measures the gentleman, if he wears a hat, removes it, and the partners prepare for and execute a prolonged bow and courtesy. They then move forward, turning to face each other with a waltz-like pivot, and make another bow and courtesy, the lady stepping to her right, and the gentleman to his left. After this they return to their places with *pas de bourrée*, giving hands as they finish. The gentleman, as he resumes his original position, brings his left foot to the *third position* behind, and the lady draws her right foot to the *third position* in front.

The partners now with their hands joined, the lady's left being held in the gentleman's right, make two *pas de menuet en avant*, each beginning with the right foot. The gentleman then makes the *pas à droite*, stepping a little backward,* while the lady passes round before him; then, releasing hands, they both continue the step to the right till they are facing each other at corners in the position to commence the *figure principale*.† In

* "*L'homme fait un pas de menuet en arrière, pour laisser passer votre demoiselle devant vous.*"—RAMEAU.

† Another contemporary writer says: "The cavalier takes his lady by the hand and makes two steps forward with her, both keeping on the same line, after which he causes her to describe a circle round him, which brings her back to the same spot whence she started."

executing these last steps the partners should keep their right shoulders back, turning the head a little to the left, so that they look towards each other.*

[NOTE.—The movements in a minuet must depend greatly on the nature of the music selected; and clearly when it is performed as a show dance the position of the partners at certain stages will be regulated by that of the audience.]

The principal figure of the minuet, which, as we have already seen, was reconstructed by the celebrated dancer Pécour from the still more ancient S figure, occupies twelve measures of the music, and is executed as follows:—

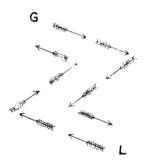

The partners first make two *pas de menuet* to the left, which bring them in a position to make the *traversé oblique*. In commencing the first of these minuet

* "*En faisant ce pas vous effacez l'un et l'autre l'épaule droite et la tête un peu tournée du côte gauche en vous regardant.*"

N

steps, the partners move a little forward, and in the
second a little backward, so that the distance between
them is not lessened. Now both make the *pas de mennet
en avant*, and in doing so they should be careful to turn
their faces towards each other, and draw back their right
shoulders as they pass. The second of these steps is
made in turning, so that the dancers are again facing.
After this they make the steps to the right, each finishing
in the position where the other began.*

[NOTE.—It appears, according to the old authorities, that the above figure might be performed an
indefinite number of times,† a fact which, I must
confess, does not appear easily reconcilable with a
due regard to coincidence of music and motion,
unless the players were supposed to watch the
movements of the dancers and repeat measures
accordingly. Anyhow we can see that a certain
amount of freedom was allowed, and in arranging

* Rameau, in one of his plates, has written the following
instructions, forming therewith the figure of a Z as shown above :
" *l'homme deux pas du côte gauche, deux pas en avant en effaçant
l'épaule, un en arrière du côte droit.*" In the parallel lines he has
written for " *la demoiselle*" the same instructions which are
amplified in the text.

† "They then cross each other during four or five minutes,
looking at each other as they pass " (old description). Rameau
in one instance says : " *Lorsque vous avez fait cinq ou six tours de
suite,*" and in another " . . . *votre figure principale que vous
continuez trois ou quatre tours*"—three, four, five, or six times.

a minuet we can safely regulate the movements so that they will best accord with the particular music selected.*]

In the next figure the partners *balancez* to give the right hand, raising it to the height of the chest. They should look towards one another, turning the head a little to the right, and a slight inclination of the body should be made in presenting the hand. Now follows a *tour entière*, or complete turn, composed of three *pas de menuet en avant*, in the third of which the partners release hands, and turn to face each other. This occupies eight measures of the music.

The partners now give the left hand to each other, and make a similar tour to the left. On releasing hands they execute the *pas de menuet à droite*, and this brings them into the position for repeating the principal figure.

Finally, the dancers present both hands and turn ; the gentleman, keeping only the right hand of the lady, releases his left in order to remove his hat, which in the course of the dance has been resumed ;† and the minuet concludes with two bows and courtesies similar to those with which it began.

* There are versions of the rather doleful music known as the *Menuet de la Cour*, which contain an odd number of bars in the second part. This makes it rather unsatisfactory for dancing purposes. There are other versions of the same music, however, which contain equal divisions of bars.

† "*Il quitte la main gauche seulement, pour en ôter du même tems son chapeau.*"

I have now, reader, presented the minuet in what I believe to be its original and correct form as a *danse de salon.* But the figures are only presented, as it were, in outline. All those numerous graces and ornaments about the execution of which there can be any doubt are purposely omitted. The elaborate *balancé,* the majestic *pas grave,* the graceful *bourrée,* the proper wrist movements and elegance of carriage requisite for the dance, can only be acquired by taking lessons of a competent instructor. But at least you may rest assured that the figures and steps here described are strictly correct. My object has been not to present an effective fancy dance, but the genuine minuet as it was performed at the court of Louis XV.

*   *   *   *   *

To the question, so frequently asked, whether the minuet is likely to be revived, I would reply:

Yes, perhaps, some day in the dim and distant future, but not until many changes have appeared in the kaleidoscope of fashion. When the garments of men are again made picturesque; when girls have ceased to bestride the bicycle; when the new woman shall have followed the path of

the dodo; when maidens no longer pose as men's
equals in all things, but are content to resume their
true position as men's superiors in the gentler
qualities only; in short, when women shall again
command that chivalrous respect and devotion of
which the dance is specially typical, and which they
have done so much of late to abolish; when
rowdyism shall be replaced by refinement; when
æsthetic tastes are generally cultivated, and dancing is once more regarded as an art—then maybe,
but not till then, will the minuet be revived as a
social pastime.

CHAPTER VIII.

MODERN DANCING.

IN these days of culture, when the public mind
is being trained to perceive and appreciate whatever is lovely in nature and art; when music is
universally studied; when pictorial skill has made
such rapid strides towards perfection that even the
illustrations in our children's toy-books are often
things of beauty; when there is ample evidence of
general improvement in taste and design in our
streets, our buildings, on the walls, and in the
furniture of our homes; when science has realised
marvels which, a few years since, would have been
deemed incredible; indeed, when everything appears
to be moving in a progressive scale, is it not strange
that a single art, one which, as we have seen, was
in classic times deemed worthy to rank with poetry
and painting—the art of dancing—has degenerated
to such an extent that its practice, as frequently
exhibited both in public and private, is a positive
disgrace to the age?

This is no exaggerated statement. It is one which I think any competent critic is hardly likely to deny. I would particularly avoid appearing to unduly disparage the dancing of my own day, or compare it unfavourably with the dancing of past times, because this is precisely what an enthusiastic writer is tempted to do, and I wish to consider the matter from a perfectly unbiassed standpoint.

The writer who considers the subject of dancing has not the same advantages as have writers upon the kindred arts. A critic who treats of painting in its various aspects can examine both ancient and modern pictures with equal facility, and, allowing for the mellowness produced by time, he can with strict impartiality compare the paintings of the present day with those of masters in past ages.

The critical writer on musical art has also a similar advantage. It is true that we know comparatively little of the practice of music in remote times, but we are at least able justly to compare the music of immediately preceding centuries with that which is composed to-day.

So is it likewise with sculpture, architecture, and

ornamental design. But the critic of dancing is, in the nature of things, tempted to become a *laudator temporis acti,* because, although the present practice of the art is before him, with all its imperfections and crudities, in addition to whatever grace it may possess, he can witness nothing in the dances of past ages to dispel his cherished dreams of what dancing should be. He sees them only through the mediums of idealised description, pictorial illustration, and tradition.

Let us take one or two examples:

The painter who produced a serious picture of modern theatrical dancing would naturally select the most artistic poses or movements for illustration. A skirt dancer, for instance, would be depicted by any artist of good taste in graceful, undulating motion or some refined and elegant posture, certainly not kicking at an imaginary object above her head. And thus some critic of future years may exclaim, " How graceful, how beautiful, how refined, must this skirt dancing have been ! " He would speak thus because he would see nothing of the inane vulgarity by which this kind of performance has been too often disfigured.

Again, our hypothetical critic in the future may

come across a picture of social dancing. Several couples may be represented as executing the movement generally known as the barn dance. The artist has naturally drawn them with their arms gracefully extended, their heads well posed, and their feet pointed downward. Our critic observes the picture, and studies a technical description of the dance. He knows the steps employed, and understands exactly how all the movements *should* have been executed, since the rules of true art always have and always will be the same. Once more he may cry out, "What an elegant dance must this barn dance have been!" He will not hear the stamping nor observe the rougher element, which seems to have become almost inseparable from such movements in actual practice.

Having, then, due regard to the above considerations, if I err in my judgment of the style of dancing which obtains at the present time in its relation to the "dancing of all ages," I would err on the side of moderation, and be disposed to take a hopeful rather than a despondent view of the present condition of the art; but unfortunately there are some evils in the modern style of dancing which call for the most unsparing condemnation.

The quality of vulgarity, in its generally accepted sense, is by no means peculiar to any particular epoch. In tracing the history of dancing, those who read between the lines, so to speak, and make due allowance for the fact that matters have been generally presented at their best, can discover evidences of vulgarity in other ages as well as our own; and we have seen that many of the dances of ancient and classic times, like the Chica and those performances of a later day prohibited by the Spanish Inquisition, were distinctly suggestive of the baser passions of humanity.

But although vulgarity is certainly not conspicuous by its absence from modern dancing (and, indeed, it is only in accordance with the fitness of things that the society which was responsible for the apotheosis of the costermonger and the glorification of the cowboy should have adopted something of the methods of its idols in its style of dancing), the charge of impropriety cannot, I think, consistently be brought against it.

We have seen in a preceding chapter how the waltz was at first denounced in the interests of public morality. Among the moralists who denounced it perhaps the most conspicuous, and certainly the most unexpected, figure was that of Lord Byron, who, under the pseudonym of Horace Hornem, published a decasyllabic poem on the subject with which all my readers are probably familiar. It would be difficult to conceive a more scathingly satirical diatribe than is presented in this "apostrophic hymn," as he termed it. But, although the publication of *The Waltz* did not deter society from indulging in its favourite pastime, it may have tended to modify the manner of its performance.

Certainly people do not nowadays whirl around like "two cockchafers spitted upon the same bodkin." They have discovered that so far as the movement is concerned greater advantage may be gained by drawing away from one another in accordance with centrifugal action than by actual bodily contact. No longer is the "stranger's hand" allowed to "wander undisplaced round all the confines of the yielded waist." He, the stranger, merely places his hand against the small of his partner's back, while a most respectful distance is observed between them.

There is some satisfaction in being able to say that if our social dancing has generally deteriorated of late years, there has at least been considerable improvement in our manner of waltzing.

Unfortunately, however, the fascination of the waltz has become so powerful that in many circles it has been permitted to invade the square dances, a condition of things which twenty years ago was peculiar to the platforms of riverside pleasure-gardens, and would not have been tolerated in decent society. This, of course, is only a matter of custom, but the practice of waltzing in square dances is to be deprecated, because, as I have elsewhere pointed out, when once people begin to waltz they never seem to know when it is time to leave off, and so the figures get distorted out of all shape.

The faithful historian of dancing will, I think, be constrained to record that the general style which characterised the closing years of the nine-teenth century was by no means improper; it was not necessarily or exceptionally vulgar, but in the main, both as regards public and private practice, it was simply idiotic.

For many years past it has seemed to be the general aim of dancers, with, of course, some honourable exceptions, to set all established rules of art at defiance. On the stage we have seen dancing degenerate into absolutely meaningless exhibitions of tumbling, kicking, and flapping of skirts; while in the ball-room it has become mere romping.

In my opening chapter I endeavoured to explain that the highest order of dancing is dramatic dancing, in which every gesture is illustrative of some phase of life. Love, joy, sorrow, rage, despair, hope, every emotion of the human heart, may be expressed by the dance. But what sentiment, I ask, is expressed by repeatedly kicking the foot up in the air? What does it *mean?* Nothing, absolutely nothing whatever. It is not beautiful; it is not clever; it is not even funny. It neither excites admiration nor laughter. True, the many who gaze may wonder at the suppleness of joint displayed, but the greatest wonder to the few who think is how people in an enlightened age can tolerate such wretched exhibitions of perverted art.

The high-kicking of the professional, and I am afraid I must add some amateur lady dancers, is analogous to stamping in the ball-room and the ridiculous practice of turning backwards in the *moulinet* figure of the Lancers, which certain male dancers adopted apparently for no other reason than a desire to outrage all laws of art, gracefulness, and even decorum.

Yet I trust it will be remembered that during this period of decadence, of which the historian of dancing must take note, there were always a few teachers who consistently resolved to impart to their pupils only what was good and beautiful in dancing, whose voices, feeble as they sounded at the time amidst the din of triumphant rowdyism, were nevertheless strong enough to carry weight, and rescue their art from the deplorable condition into which it had for the time fallen.

Let it also be remembered that there were a few professional dancers who, possessing the conscious power of performing all those lovely steps and movements which belong to Terpsichore's legitimate domain—*the very names of which are almost unknown to the modern theatrical critic*—resolutely refused to pander to a depraved public taste for movements which have no connection whatever with the real art of dancing, but can only be rightly included with the arts of the acrobat and the contortionist.

I feel convinced, however, that the deterioration
of stage dancing, which during the past decade
has been so apparent to competent judges, is only
a passing phase of an art which has already
survived many similar periods of decline. Even
about the confusion of dancing with acrobatic
performances there is nothing new. Many of us
have seen a curious old illustration representing
Salome dancing upon her head, and though there
is not the slightest probability that this accomplishment was included in the lady's *repertoire*, it
certainly represents the artist's idea of what kind
of movements were most likely to charm the
beholder. Again, we have seen in an earlier
chapter how Hippocleides lost the hand of
Agarista, not through genuine dancing, but because he allowed his dancing to degenerate into
mere tumbling.

Owen Jones, in his *Grammar of Ornament*, points
out how during the best periods of art the leaves
and flowers, from which ideas of ornamentation
are derived, appear in a strictly conventionalised
form, while in periods of decline they are represented in almost their natural state. I think it
is much the same with the steps employed in

dancing. When the art is in a high state of perfection, the movements of the limbs are subjected to rigidly conventional rules, the steps become intricate and brilliant, and are of a nature to dazzle the eye. As dancing degenerates, however, the movements become more primitive, there is less regard to light and shade, the extensions of limbs become more pronounced, and there is a general lack of refinement. But the art must indeed have sunk to a low ebb when the applause of an audience can be excited by mere ability to imitate a notable characteristic of the mule.

There has, however, been some improvement in theatrical dancing during the past few years. The "kick," the "split," and the "cart-wheel," as these antics are termed, are now generally only exhibited at inferior places of entertainment, while at the best theatres there seems already to be a demand for something superior. The kind of dance in which a flowing skirt is used as the chief accessory may, of course, be made a thing of real beauty when arranged in accordance with artistic principles, and performed by a dancer who happens to possess a true sense of the poetry of pose and motion. But every movement of the arms must be regulated according to the conditions of art, harmoniously with the action of the feet, and should be of such a nature that it would present a pleasing appearance even if the skirt were not held. This kind of dancing is admirably adapted for drawing-room performance, but the professional dancer who wished to please a critical and enlightened public— assuming that dancing should again be studied and appreciated as an art—would have to practise something more than the movements required for skirt dancing. She would have to practise her *entrechats, caprioles, ailles de pigeons,* and all those beautiful and brilliant steps which belong to the classic school, and are now so rarely exhibited in perfection.

As regards dancing in its social aspects, it must be admitted that the prospect is not particularly encouraging. Dr. Max Nordau, after showing what an extremely important affair dancing has been in times long past, declares that it is to-day " no more than a fleeting pastime for women and youths, and later on its last atavistic survival will be the dancing of children."*

Whatever may be our opinion of Dr. Nordau's

* MAX NORDAU, *Degeneration.*

O

prognostications with regard to the future of the
arts generally—and it might not be difficult to
show that they are mostly in a state of advancement rather than decadence – it is impossible to
combat his assertion with regard to the special
art we are now considering. An impartial observer
who watched a performance of the "Kitchen
Lancers," especially if he remembered the figures
as they were danced twenty years since, would
hardly think our progress in social dancing was a
matter of which we had much occasion to be proud.
Every innovation introduced into the Lancers had
been a further deformity, until at length the
manner of performing the figures became such that
many ladies of good taste refused to join in the
dance, while hostesses sometimes thought it wiser
to exclude it from their programmes.

Then comes the inevitable change. Among the
higher classes of society, ball-room rowdyism (there
is no other word expressive of this style of dancing)
is decidedly on the wane, but it is succeeded by
apathy. Fashionable life, according to Mr. Herbert
Spencer, "is not passed in being happy, but in
playing at being happy."* And in the ball-room

* *Study of Sociology.*

it is not real pleasure that is produced by dancing of an inferior order, but only make-believe pleasure. Dancing is not enjoyable unless it is good, and the only way to enjoy dancing is to learn to dance properly. The rules of dancing, like the rules of any other pastime, should be studied and obeyed. Society will not do this. It contents itself with "playing at being happy" in the ball-room for a while, and then becomes bored with the inanity of the whole proceeding.

It might have been expected that when the teaching of dancing was relegated more particularly to lady professors, as it has been of late years, its practice as a social pursuit would have been characterised by increased refinement; but we have seen that the actual result has been precisely of an opposite nature. As a matter of fact, the teachers have devoted far too much time to gymnastic exercises and skirt drill, and far too little to genuine dancing. The figures of square dances make some demand upon the memory, and in the ball-room men have always been more or less remiss with regard to this matter. But formerly, when any hesitancy occurred, their partners were able to help them out of the difficulty; and, having learnt to appreciate the movements in their correct form, they naturally inclined to adopt them. Now, however, neither partner knows what ought to be done, so they simply *do anything,* and the result is hopeless confusion.

It must, I think, be admitted that not a little of the marked deterioration of ball-room manners has resulted from the attitude lately adopted by a large section of women. The desire which they have evinced to emancipate themselves from conventional restraint, and live and act on strict equality with men, has led to a diminution of that graceful and chivalrous courtesy which the true gentleman has hitherto always shown to the presumably weaker creature who has relied on him for protection. Whatever a man's real feelings may be, he does not now generally express himself as being "honoured" or "favoured" by a lady's companionship. He simply asks her to dance in much the same manner as he would ask a male friend to have a drink. It would have seemed incredible some years since that a man should dare, in any decent ball-room, to drag his partner backwards in dancing, or attempt to swing her off her feet. But we have seen this kind of thing done

in places where one would least expect to en-
counter rowdyism in any form. Certain it is that
girls nowadays, at least the majority of them, will
cheerfully submit to treatment which their mothers
probably, and their grandmothers certainly, would
have indignantly resented.

The general condition of dancing as a social
pursuit is, I think, now such that ere long one of
two things must inevitably happen. Either we
may look for some very pronounced improvement
in its practice, or it will gradually, and for a time,
fall into disuse, as was the case in the Middle Ages.
That dancing, whatever may be its present fate,
will eventually revive, there can be little doubt,
seeing that a love of bodily rhythmic movement
is inherent in our nature, and perhaps in its
regeneration the art may reach to higher forms
of development than any that have yet been
conceived.

But, as I recently stated, there are not wanting
signs of a growing distaste for desultory dancing
in the ball-room. It may be that there are already
manifestations of a tendency towards improvement
in the practice of the art; but the day of its
regeneration as a refining influence on the minds

and manners of youth, the day when it will resume something of the importance it held among the Dorians, will not dawn until it is generally taught by men and women of cultivated intellect and taste.

It is not, however, to teachers alone that we must look for the work of regeneration. They can accomplish but little unless the public mind awakens to the fact that whether we are disposed to regard dancing as a fine art, or merely as a graceful and agreeable pastime, the nearer its practice approaches perfection the greater will be the pleasure derivable therefrom.

*   *   *   *   *

I have now attempted briefly to show what dancing has been, what it is, and what it should be. My readers may be numerous or few; but whether they reach to hundreds merely, or to thousands, it may be safely assumed that all will be more or less interested in the subject. Many may deplore the present degenerate condition of dancing, and wish that they could further the work of improvement. If, then, each one would earnestly endeavour to exert his or her influence in the right direction, doubtless some good result would follow. Teachers, with ideals sufficiently lofty, might form resolutions to sink all personal jealousies, and work harmoniously together for the amelioration of their art. Readers who are past their dancing days might use their eloquence in dissuading younger folks from indulging in unseemly antics. Young men might resolve to praise and applaud only what was good and beautiful in dancing when exhibited on the stage, and seek by persuasion and example to reform the practices and manners of the ball-room. Girls might hint to their partners that they preferred to dance in a quiet and orderly manner, and I doubt if any men with the slightest pretensions to being considered gentlemen would venture to disregard their wishes. Above all, mothers, to whom I would commend a thoughtful perusal of Dr. Arabella Kenealy's article on "Woman as an Athlete,"* may help in the work of regeneration by resolutely insisting that their children, and daughters especially, shall be taught *genuine dancing* by experienced and cultured professors, who understand not merely the steps and figures of dances, but know how to impart the true

* *Nineteenth Century Magazine,* April, 1899.

grammar and technique of their art, with all those
beautiful arm movements and exercises of body and
limb that properly belong thereto. Dancing, when
really well taught, is invaluable as an aid to physical
development in girls, bringing as it does every part
of the body into graceful and harmonious action,
without undue muscular strain.

It would indeed be a regrettable circumstance
if dancing were to fall into permanent or even
temporary disuse, but the former contingency at
least there is little reason to fear. In considering
the period of its decadence, I have been constrained
to adopt a somewhat pessimistic tone, but would
fain conclude by expressing the hope, nay, conviction, that dancing will sooner or later resume
its ancient dignity, and be once more regarded not
as a frivolous pastime, not merely as a recreative
art, but as an art by which natural loveliness may
be enhanced and life adorned.

INDEX

PLYMOUTH :
WILLIAM BRENDON AND SON, PRINTERS.

Printed in the United Kingdom
by Lightning Source UK Ltd.
115360UKS00001B/59